FIRST EDITION

PENNSYLVANIA GOVERNMENT AND POLITICS

By John J. Kennedy

Bassim Hamadeh, CEO and Publisher
Kassie Graves, Director of Acquisitions and Sales
Jamie Giganti, Senior Managing Editor
Jess Estrella, Senior Graphic Designer
John Remington, Senior Field Acquisitions Editor
Monika Dziamka, Project Editor
Brian Fahey, Senior Licensing Specialist
Christian Berk, Associate Production Editor
Joyce Lue, Interior Designer

Printed in the United States of America

ISBN: 978-1-5165-0158-8 (pbk) / 978-1-5165-0159-5 (br)

To my mom and the memory of my dad

CONTENTS

List of Tables

List of Figures

List of Maps

List of Boxes

PREFACE

The idea for this book was planted roughly ten years ago, after I first began teaching a course on Pennsylvania Politics at West Chester University. It's a class that I enjoy probably more than any other, and I've been fortunate to offer it as part of our Political Science Department's Legislative Fellow Program. This has enabled state legislators to periodically come into the classroom and serve as joint instructors of the class with me. One problem I encountered, however, was that there really wasn't an appropriate textbook to cover Pennsylvania's government system. *The Pennsylvania Manual*, published by the Department of State in the commonwealth, provided some important relative information, but it wasn't the type of book that students could really read through as text. I did use Historian Paul Beers's landmark book *Pennsylvania Politics, Today and Yesterday*, and while that gave the class a tremendous amount of information on many of the historical figures in the state and students always enjoyed his colorful writing style and humorous anecdotes, the book itself was written forty years ago and still left a vacuum as far as statistical data and specific information on the government structures of the state. In conjunction with Beers's book, the class also used one that I wrote, *Pennsylvania Elections*, which was originally published in 2004 and revised a decade later. While it may have filled the data gap as it pertained to elections in the state, it still did not address such areas as the state's governmental institutions and processes.

That finally changed two years ago when, in the process of wrapping up the revised edition of my elections book and pondering what to do next, John Remington of Cognella Books walked into my office one spring afternoon and asked whether I had any projects in mind for possible publication. After a long chat, we agreed to pursue a project that would eventually lead to this, *Pennsylvania Government and Politics*. We decided that the book should potentially serve as both a stand-alone text for a class in Pennsylvania politics or as a supplement for American Government or State and Local Government classes.

That being considered, I've had two audiences in mind in the process of writing this book. The first is my students and those of other colleges and universities across the state; my hope is to provide them with a basic overview of the governmental institutions in the state, comparisons that show how our state compares with others on a host of issues, and some updated statistical pieces relating election results and political trends. The other audience is composed of those like myself, interested in our state government, who finally have what I hope to be a miniature textbook on Pennsylvania's government, one that almost every other state has seen published but one that this state had not been able to benefit from. I do hope that it satisfies that purpose.

I want to thank those at Cognella Academic Publishing, in particular John Remington, for offering me this opportunity, and Monika Dziamka, who guided me through it. Additionally, I would like to express my gratitude towards each of the state lawmakers who've come to my classes and help educate all of us on the intricate ways of the Pennsylvania political system. I'd like to also acknowledge my students, whose curiosities continue to motivate me to be the best professor that I can. Also, my colleagues in the Department of Political Science at West Chester University, especially our Department Chair, Dr. Frauke Schnell, and Dr. Peter Loedel for their support in matters relating to this project and others. Also, administrative assistant Tara Easterling, who keeps me organized at the office and lets me know when I need to replace the office water bottle. Finally, Beau Ryck, a graduate student in the Geography Department, for doing such a great job in creating the various maps.

Foremost, however, I want to thank my family. My mother, Helen Kennedy, who continues to serve as an inspiration for all who are fortunate to know her, and to my father, Robert Kennedy, who as my role model exemplified all the finest values. To both I've dedicated this book. To my wife, Kelli, who has been my best friend since we first met in a summer class back in 1982, and to our beautiful daughters, Clare and Shannon, that their interest in politics only continues to grow.

John J. Kennedy, February 2017

1 A PROFILE OF PENNSYLVANIA

THE KEYSTONE STATE

There is a reason Pennsylvania is known as the "Keystone State." That's because no other state was as central to the development of the United States of America as was the Commonwealth of Pennsylvania.

Its story is well known. It begins with a founder, William Penn, who established the principle of freedom of religious conviction that would serve as a model throughout the rest of the New World. It was in the state's largest city, Philadelphia, that the nation's independence was forged in the summer of 1776. It was in that same city, and that same place, eleven years later, in what would later become known as Independence Hall, that the Grand Experiment of our representative democracy was launched.

Three-fourths of a century later, the critical battle in this country's most serious conflict was decided here, when the tide of the Confederate Army was rolled back—and the Union itself was preserved—just outside the town of Gettysburg. After the Civil War, it was again Pennsylvania that would generate the power of an Industrial Revolution in the United States. This transformation occurred throughout the commonwealth, manifest in steel stacks of the Monongahela Valley in the southwestern part of the state; in the northwest, where the nation's first oil well was drilled; in the anthracite coal mines of the northeast; and in the manufacturing plants and textile mills of the Lehigh Valley. And of course, we cannot forget what was and still remains the commonwealth's number one industry, agriculture, which has served as the breadbasket for both state and nation throughout our shared history.

As it pertains to the "Commonwealth" title itself, Pennsylvania is still referred to as such, though that and the title "state" are now used interchangeably. The term itself is of English derivation and refers to the idea of a group of citizens united for some common purpose; however, the title itself bears no exact legal significance. The designation of commonwealth was established in the Constitution of 1776, and it has been carried forth in each successive one that has followed. Three other states (Kentucky, Massachusetts, and Virginia) also use the label to define themselves.

Table 1.1 below lists a number of other Pennsylvania symbols, some of which are fairly well known, while others are rather obscure.

Table 1.1 Pennsylvania State Symbols

STATE ANIMAL	WHITETAIL DEER
State Game Bird	Ruffed Grouse
State Dog	Great Dane
State Fish	Brook Trout
State Flower	Mountain Laurel
State Insect	Firefly
State Beverage	Milk
State Tree	Hemlock
State Ship	United States Niagara
State Plant	Penngift Crownvetch
State Fossil	Phacops rana
State Steam Locomotive	Pennsylvania Railroad K4
State Electric Locomotive	Pennsylvania Railroad GG1

THE PENNSYLVANIA CULTURE

Despite the integration of American society today towards a more national culture, differences still exist across the fifty states: life in Pennsylvania is not the same as life in Maine, or Alabama, or Wyoming. The particular culture of a state, established through its history, geography, economics, and racial and ethnic mix, to name a few, creates a political system that is unique to itself. It is therefore important to understand a state's political culture in order to fully examine the policies and type of government that exist in any individual state.

Political culture can best be defined as "the set of attitudes, beliefs, behavior, and sentiments that gives order and meaning to a political process." These attitudes, drawn from experiences, give people a set of "underlying assumptions and rules that govern individual and group behavior in a political system. They guide political behavior by articulating what is proper and what is acceptable."[1] Still the most comprehensive effort to evaluate and categorize American political culture is Daniel J. Elazar's groundbreaking research, conducted several decades ago, which divided states nationally according to three different types: *moralistic*, *traditionalistic*, and *individualistic*. Each of these three subcultures is grounded in conflicting perceptions of how the political arena is to be organized, how power is to be held and exercised, and how justice is to be achieved.[2]

The *moralistic* political culture sprung from the Puritan settlements of New England, with an emphasis on a commonwealth view of government and society. Politics is viewed in this culture as a worthy pursuit that should benefit the public good and be above private interests. Every citizen has a responsibility to participate in the governing of the community—a philosophy that served as the foundation of what would become the New England town meeting. Government agencies should be organized to promote the efficient delivery of public services and should be staffed by professional administrators, not those with political agendas. Stretching out across New England, the *moralistic* culture spread across the northern tier of the Upper Midwest and Great Lakes region and into the Wheat Belt, the Rocky Mountain states, and the upper northwest of the nation.

The *traditionalistic* political culture arose in the Southern colonies, which relied on indentured labor and slaves to maintain their agrarian, manorial lifestyle. Those at the top of the socioeconomic ladder asserted a dominant role in the politics of the community, and power was restricted to a small circle of elite families. Governments functioned primarily as a means of maintaining *traditional* values and defending the status quo. From the Coastal Southeast, the *traditionalistic* culture spread throughout the Old Confederacy and across the southwest part of the United States.

The *individualistic* culture, which is how Pennsylvania is categorized, is one in which the citizens tend to view the political arena as a marketplace. Political parties and politicians compete to provide services and are compensated, whether in the form of patronage or simply of power. Political leaders, who are often professionals, are expected to personally gain from their efforts, and citizens have a high tolerance for corruption. Party loyalty is important and used for the exchange of influence, whether though patronage or other preferments. The *individualistic* culture developed in the colonies of the Mid-Atlantic, including Pennsylvania, then spread into the Corn Belt and, finally, across the Central Plains states. Though these subcultures have been diluted somewhat by migration as we have become a more mobile society, it does provide a good starting point for analyzing and understanding the development of a state's institutions and the behavior, outlook, and expectations of the citizens themselves.

Certainly, the reputation that Pennsylvania has attained as a breeding ground of corruption is not unwarranted. In fact, one recent study conducted by researchers at Indiana University concluded that the state ranked fifth nationally in their "corruption index." Corruption has long been a part of the state's culture.[3] Noted Pennsylvania historian Paul Beers cited US Senators Matthew Quay and Boise Penrose as the principals in establishing a breeding ground for graft that began in the late 1800s. Infamously, after the original capitol building was rebuilt after being destroyed by fire in 1897, cost overruns and bloated budgetary items ultimately led to five convictions, including the chief architect, as well nine other indictments and three purported suicides.[4]

The decade of the 1970s was another particularly troubling era as state government turned a blind eye toward honesty and ethics. During the administration of Governor Milton Shapp, seven lawmakers, including House Speaker Herbert Fineman as well as eleven high party officials, were convicted of corruption of one sort or another. This prompted five former prosecutors to launch campaigns to succeed Shapp, and ultimately it was a major reason why Richard Thornburgh, the Allegheny County district attorney, was successful.[5]

Image 1.1 US Senator Boies Penrose

The next several decades were relatively quiet by Pennsylvania standards, but they were not exempt from scandal. Statewide officials such as Auditor-General Al Benedict and Attorney General Ernie Preate both went to prison. Most tragically, however, Budd Dwyer, the state auditor-general who had earlier defeated Benedict, shot himself in the head in front of a host of television cameras on the eve of his sentencing on corruption charges. After a bit of a lull, things started anew in the mid-2000s, so much so that someone could write a book about it—and in fact, someone did: reporter Brad Bumsted's *Keystone Corruption*, published in 2013. One of the most notorious scandals in recent years was "Bonusgate," in which it was alleged that close to $4 million was handed out as bonuses to legislative staffers for illegally doing campaign work while on the state payroll. The probe itself was spearheaded by State Attorney General Tom Corbett, who parlayed it straight to the governor's mansion after having snared a number of prominent officials from both sides of the aisle, including Republican house speaker John Perzel and Democratic house minority leader William DeWeese.[6]

More recently, the state witnessed State Treasurer Rob McCord resign after being charged with extortion in an effort to raise money for his 2014 bid for the Democratic nomination for governor. Attorney General Kathleen Kane, once seen as a rising star in the Democratic Party, recently witnessed her political career come crashing down in the aftermath of numerous complaints about actions that ranged from leaking grand jury testimony to failure to prosecute several Philadelphia legislators for allegedly taking bribes. In August 2016, she was ultimately convicted on several charges, the most serious of which was felony perjury, which led to her being sentenced to two years in prison. Efforts to investigate Kane's dealings ultimately led to more scandal, specifically what would become known as "Porngate," in which it was found that a number of prominent state employees were exchanging a number of emails that were considered pornographic, racist, or misogynist. The trial led to the judicial branch and the state supreme court itself, prompting two of the justices to resign in disgrace. This followed a few years after another justice on the state's highest court resigned after having been found guilty of felony by theft of services. In other words, within a period of a few years, three of the state's seven justices on the state's highest court resigned from office. Again, a chronology of this state's corruption has literally filled a book, and likely a second edition.

POPULATION

From 1950 to 2012, the population of the United States increased from 161,325,798 to 312,780,968. During that time, the populations of most states grew as well. Several states, primarily located in the Sun Belt, even doubled in population. However, several other states, mostly in the North, had stagnant growth. One such state is Pennsylvania.

In 1950, Pennsylvania ranked as the third most populous state in the nation (behind New York and California), with a total of 10,498,012 inhabitants. It now ranks sixth, surpassed by three additional states: two in the Sun Belt (Texas in 1980 and Florida in 1987) and one in the Midwest, Illinois, which inched ahead of Pennsylvania in the 2000 census. The total population of Pennsylvania, according to the most recent figures available, is now 12,763,536 (Table 1.2), an increase of just two million inhabitants in a little over sixty years. The political implications of this are many, from the loss of productive capacity in the private sector to the weakening of political clout in the public sector. When Dwight Eisenhower carried the state in the presidential election of 1952, Pennsylvania handed him its thirty-two electoral votes. In the most recent contest, Donald Trump could only claim twenty electoral votes, a 44 percent decline, though they were certainly important.

The population has also shifted within the commonwealth, increasing in some areas while declining in others. As Table 1.3 illustrates, the most updated figures provided by the US Census Bureau indicate that five of the top seven most populated counties in the state are located in the southeast region. These include Philadelphia, the largest city in the state, which comprises 12 percent of the overall total, followed by Montgomery (third ranked, 6.3 percent overall), Bucks (fourth, 4.9 percent), Delaware (fifth, 4.4 percent), and Chester (seventh, 3.0 percent). Together, these four counties account for almost one-third (31.5 percent) of the overall population in the commonwealth. If the three counties of Berks, Lehigh, and Northampton, essentially exurbs of Philadelphia and also part of its media market, are included, the number rises to almost 40 percent.

In the southwest, Allegheny County, which contains the second-largest city, Pittsburgh, is also the second-largest county, with almost 10 percent of its population. Lancaster and York Counties, located along the Maryland state border, rank sixth and eighth, respectively, while Westmoreland County, adjacent to Allegheny in the west, rounds out the top ten. At the other end of the population spectrum are the ten most sparsely populated counties, with most located in the northern half of the state's geographic area; the exceptions are Juniata and Fulton Counties, located in the south-central region along the Susquehanna River, and Greene County, located at the southwesterly tip of the state.

In addition, through the period between 2000–2010, twenty-nine of the state's sixty-seven counties lost population, with the vast majority of those in either the west or the rural northern tier. In fact, twenty-four of the twenty-seven counties that lie west of Centre County, which is in the exact middle of the state, lost population in the last decade. The exceptions are Butler,

Table 1.2 Pennsylvania's Population Since 1950

YEAR	POPULATION		YEAR	POPULATION		YEAR	POPULATION
2016	12,811,239						
2015	12,802,503		**1993**	12,030,079		**1971**	11,879,000
2014	12,793,767		**1992**	11,995,405		**1970**	11,793,909
2013	12,783,536		**1991**	11,961,070		**1969**	11,803,000
2012	12,763,536		**1990**	11,881,643		**1968**	11,755,400
2011	12,742,886		**1989**	12,040,102		**1967**	11,646,000
2010	12,702,379		**1988**	12,002,236		**1966**	11,637,900
2009	12,604,767		**1987**	11,936,396		**1965**	11,535,200
2008	12,448,279		**1986**	11,889,165		**1964**	11,459,000
2007	12,432,792		**1985**	11,863,672		**1963**	11,424,000
2006	12,440,621		**1984**	11,900,701		**1962**	11,376,000
2005	12,429,616		**1983**	11,894,700		**1961**	11,468,000
2004	12,406,292		**1982**	11,885,330		**1960**	11,319,366
2003	12,365,455		**1981**	11,870,960		**1959**	11,323,000
2002	12,335,091		**1980**	11,863,895		**1958**	11,101,000
2001	12,287,150		**1979**	11,730,500		**1957**	11,166,000
2000	12,281,054		**1978**	11,749,900		**1956**	11,132,000
1999	11,994,016		**1977**	11,785,200		**1955**	11,132,000
1998	12,001,451		**1976**	11,862,000		**1954**	10,895,800
1997	12,019,661		**1975**	11,828,200		**1953**	10,829,100
1996	12,056,112		**1974**	11,835,400		**1952**	10,733,700
1995	12,071,842		**1973**	11,902,000		**1951**	10,594,900
1994	12,052,410		**1972**	11,926,000		**1950**	10,498,012

Source: The 1950, 1960, 1970, 1980, 1990, 2000 and 2010 populations as enumerated by the US Bureau of the Census. The 1981 through 1989, 1991 through 1999, 2001 through 2009, 2011 and 2012 estimated populations as prepared by the State Data Center of the Pennsylvania State University at Harrisburg. The estimated populations for all of the other years were prepared by the Pennsylvania Office of State Planning and Development.

Sources: Pennsylvania Vital Statistics Annual Report, 2012. Pennsylvania Department of Health. US Department of Census. 2010.

Forest, and Washington Counties, each of which showed a slight increase in population. Allegheny County experienced the most precipitous drop of over 58,000 residents, an almost 5 percent decline in one decade. Tiny Cameron County registered the largest decline percentagewise at 18 percent, after losing almost one thousand residents in the last ten years.

Table 1.3 Population and Rank of Pennsylvania Counties

COUNTY	TOTAL POPULATION
Philadelphia	1,526,006
Allegheny	1,223,348
Montgomery	799,874
Bucks	625,249
Delaware	558,979
Lancaster	519,445
Chester	498,886
York	434,972
Berks	411,442
Westmoreland	365,169
Lehigh	349,497
Luzerne	320,918
Northampton	297,735
Erie	280,566
Dauphin	268,100
Cumberland	235,100
Lackawanna	214,437
Washington	207,820
Butler	183,862
Beaver	170,539
Monroe	169,842
Centre	153,990
Franklin	149,618
Schuylkill	148,289
Cambria	143,679
Fayette	136,606
Lebanon	133,568
Blair	127,089
Lycoming	116,111
Mercer	116,638

(*Continued*)

Table 1.3 (*Continued*)

COUNTY	TOTAL POPULATION
Adams	101,610
Northumberland	94,528
Lawrence	91,108
Indiana	88,880
Crawford	88,765
Clearfield	81,642
Somerset	77,742
Armstrong	68,941
Columbia	67,295
Carbon	65,249
Bradford	62,622
Pike	57,369
Venango	54,984
Wayne	52,822
Bedford	49,762
Mifflin	46,682
Huntingdon	45,913
Perry	45,969
Jefferson	45,200
Union	44,947
McKean	43,450
Susquehanna	43,356
Tioga	41,981
Warren	41,815
Snyder	39,702
Clarion	39,988
Clinton	39,238
Greene	38,686
Elk	31,948
Wyoming	28,276
Juniata	24,535

Table 1.3 (*Continued*)

COUNTY	TOTAL POPULATION
Montour	18,267
Potter	17,457
Fulton	14,845
Forest	7,716
Sullivan	6,428
Cameron	5,085

Source: United States Department of Census. 2016.

sixty-five thousand more residents (a 13 percent increase), while Pike, adjacent to both the states of New Jersey and New York, was the fastest-growing county in the last decade, with an increase of over eleven thousand residents, a 19 percent increase. Even Philadelphia County enjoyed an increase, albeit slight, of about ten thousand residents, the first decade since the 1950s that its population moved in a positive direction.

Philadelphia currently ranks fifth nationally—behind New York, Los Angeles, Chicago, and Houston—with approximately 1.5 million inhabitants. That is a half-million fewer residents than 1950, when it was positioned as the third largest in the nation behind only New York and Chicago. Pittsburgh, the second-largest city in the state, has experienced an even steeper drop in its overall percentage. Its population of three hundred thousand is slightly less than half of what it was after the 1950 census. Not surprisingly, its national rank has fallen considerably, from twelfth to sixty-second nationally. Only two other cities in Pennsylvania rank among the nation's top three hundred, with Allentown checking in at 224 (population 118,000), and Erie at 291 (population 100,000). Along with their adjacent counties, together they serve as the predominant base of the commonwealth's population.

After the 2010 census, 78.7 percent of Pennsylvanians resided in urban areas, while 21.3 percent lived in rural areas. According to the Pennsylvania State Data Center, urban areas include densely developed territory and encompass residential, commercial, and other nonresidential urban land uses that meet minimum population density requirements. Additionally, urban areas are divided into two different types: "urbanized areas" of fifty thousand or more people and "urban clusters" of at least 2,500 and fewer than fifty thousand people. "Rural" encompasses all areas not considered part of an urban area. Of the 78.7 percent of urban dwellers, 89.9 percent of the population resided in urbanized areas and 10.1 percent inside urban clusters. In addition, of the state's sixty-seven counties, only one, Philadelphia, had no rural residents at all, while four, Forest, Fulton, Potter and Sullivan, did not have any urban residents. The remaining sixty-two counties had some type of urban/rural mix, with thirty-six counties having greater than 50 percent or more urbanites.

One final measure of population that the United States Bureau of the Census employs is the Standard Metropolitan Statistical Area (SMSA) delineation to measure urban growth. It defines an SMSA as a city with a population of fifty thousand or more or an urbanized area with a population of at least fifty thousand, provided that the component counties have a population of at least one hundred thousand. Of the 381 SMSAs currently identified by the Census Bureau in the United States, Pennsylvania is home to fourteen (Table 1.4). Of course, the Philadelphia SMSA ranks highest, containing the state's largest city as well as five other Pennsylvania counties, seven counties from New Jersey, two from Delaware, and even one from Maryland. Its overall population of 7.5 million places it seventh nationally. This is almost a doubling of the region's size since 1950, though this is mainly due to the geographic sprawl of the metro area. Sixty years ago, only five counties in Pennsylvania and three in New Jersey were considered part of it.

Table 1.4 Pennsylvania Standard Metropolitan Statistical Areas

STANDARD METROPOLITAN STATISTICAL AREAS	POPULATION
Philadelphia-Camden-Wilmington, PA-NJ-DE-MD Metro Area	6,051,170
Pittsburgh, PA Metro Area	2,355,968
Allentown-Bethlehem-Easton, PA-NJ Metro Area	829,835
Scranton–Wilkes-Barre–Hazleton, PA Metro Area	559,679
Harrisburg-Carlisle, PA Metro Area	560,849
Lancaster, PA Metro Area	533,320
York-Hanover, PA Metro Area	440,755
Reading, PA Metro Area	413,691
Erie, PA Metro Area	278,443
Johnstown, PA Metro Area	137,732
State College, PA Metro Area	158,742
Altoona, PA Metro Area	125,955
Youngstown, OH-Sharon, PA Metro Area	553,263
Williamsport, PA Metro Area	116,508

Source: United States Department of Census. 2010.

The second-largest SMSA is centered in Pittsburgh, and, like the city itself, it has declined by about two hundred thousand inhabitants since 1950. However, its overall size, slightly less than 2.4 million, places it twenty-second in the nation, considerably higher than Pittsburgh's standing itself among fellow cities. Like the Philadelphia SMSA, it also stretches out to include counties from a pair of additional states, two in West Virginia and one in Ohio. In 1950, it

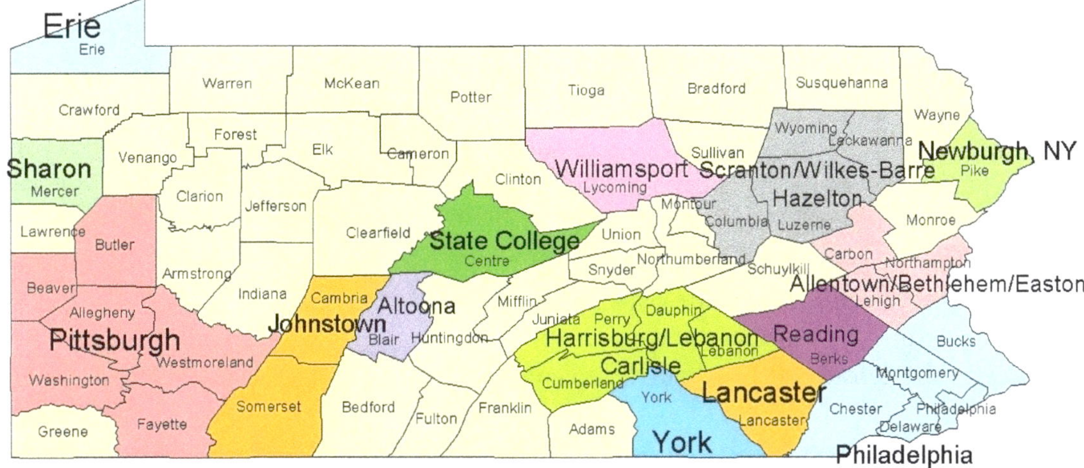

Map 1.1 Pennsylvania Standard Metropolitan Statistical Areas
Found online at http://www.sciencengines.com/mapping.php

encompassed just four Pennsylvania counties, which have now increased to five, including, most recently, Indiana County.

The third-largest SMSA in Pennsylvania, the Lehigh Valley, is also the fastest growing in the state, with a population of over 820,000. It includes Carbon, Lehigh, and Northampton Counties as well as Warren County in New Jersey, and it ranks sixty-eighth nationally. Further geographic dispersion can be observed by an increase in the number of SMSA regions in the state, which has grown from twelve in 1960 to fifteen in 1990. The most recently created SMSAs include Beaver, Sharon, State College, and Williamsport. In the latest census, however, the Scranton and Wilkes-Barre areas were combined into one grouping, reducing the overall number to fourteen.

Nevertheless, the most dramatic change to occur in recent years has been the population migration to the suburban Philadelphia region. Since 1960, the combined population of Chester, Bucks, Delaware, and Montgomery Counties has increased from 1,589,011 to 2,143,332, which now translates to 18 percent of the state's population. This shift to the southeast suburbs has affected a variety of sectors, not the least of which is political, the implications of which will be addressed throughout the book.

RACE

Although Pennsylvania's white population increased slightly in overall numbers, it has declined as a proportion of the total population to 83.4 percent (10,655,948). Meanwhile, the overall black population increased to 1,456,977 in 2012, which constitutes 11.4 percent overall of the state's total, up from 6.1 percent in 1950. Those of Hispanic origin in the most recent count numbered 781,202, which is also 6.1 percent overall today. Since census data has only tracked Hispanics more recently, any comparison over time is difficult. The same is true for Asians, which as a group make up 3.1 percent of the state overall. According to the census, this is about 1 percent more than multiracial identifiers.

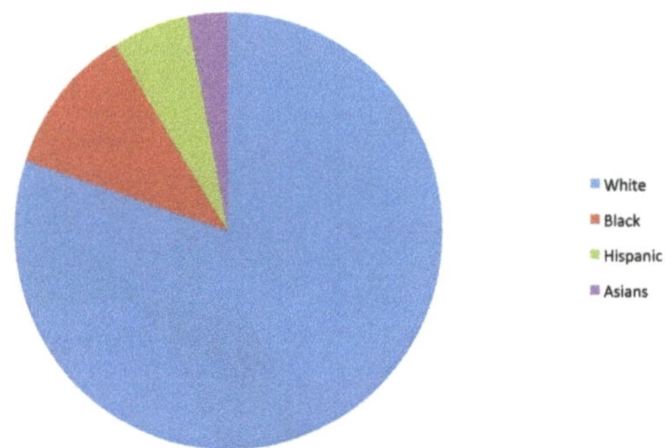

Figure 1.1 Pennsylvania Racial Composition

The overall percentage of African Americans who reside in Pennsylvania places the state twentieth nationally. A majority of Pennsylvania's black residents reside within the city of Philadelphia (56.4 percent) and, when combined with Allegheny County, contain 69.4 percent of the statewide total. In fact, those two counties, plus Delaware and Montgomery together, are home to 84.9 percent of all African Americans in the state. Within Philadelphia, blacks account for 43.6 percent, Hispanics 12.3 percent, and Asians 6.3 percent of that city's population. In Allegheny County, the totals for those three groups are 14.4 percent, 1.3 percent, and 2.0 percent, respectively. Within Pittsburgh, the second-largest city in the state, located within Allegheny County, the totals are 26.1 percent, 2.3 percent, and 4.4 percent (Table 1.5).

The number of citizens of Hispanic origin who reside in Pennsylvania place the state fourteenth nationally in that group's overall numbers, although its roughly 6 percent share ranks it only thirty-third percentagewise, as compared to the rest of the nation. Also, unlike nationally, where those of Mexican background form the largest bloc of Hispanics, the majority of Hispanic Pennsylvania residents are of Puerto Rican descent (66 percent). Those of Mexican (9 percent) and Dominican (5 percent) origin follow. The overall Asian population in the state is less than the national average of 5.6 percent, and it ranks twenty-first in total numbers. Individuals of Indian origin make up the largest share of Asians in the state, followed by those whose background are Chinese, Korean, Vietnamese, Filipino, and Japanese. This contrasts somewhat with the national breakdown, where Chinese and Filipinos rank at the top.

Table 1.5 Racial Composition of Pennsylvania Counties

COUNTY	WHITE	BLACK OR AFRICAN AMERICAN	AMERICAN INDIAN & ALASKA NATIVE	ASIAN	NATIVE HAWAIIAN & OTHER PACIFIC ISLANDER	SOME OTHER RACE	TWO OR MORE RACES	HISPANIC OR LATINO
Statewide	81.9	10.8	0.2	2.7	0	2.4	1.9	5.7
Adams	93.7	1.5	0.2	0.7	0	2.5	1.3	6
Allegheny	81.5	13.2	0.1	2.8	0	0.5	1.8	1.6
Armstrong	98	0.8	0.1	0.2	0	0.1	0.8	0.5
Beaver	91.2	6.3	0.1	0.4	0	0.2	1.7	1.2
Bedford	98	0.5	0.2	0.2	0	0.3	0.8	0.9
Berks	83.2	4.9	0.3	1.3	0	7.8	2.5	16.4
Blair	96.2	1.7	0.1	0.6	0	0.2	1.2	1
Bradford	97.5	0.5	0.2	0.5	0	0.2	1	1.1
Bucks	89.2	3.6	0.2	3.8	0	1.5	1.7	4.3
Butler	96.6	1.1	0.1	1	0	0.3	0.9	1.1
Cambria	94.1	3.6	0.1	0.5	0	0.4	1.2	1.4
Cameron	98.3	0.3	0.3	0.3	0	0.1	0.8	0.4
Carbon	95.8	1.5	0.2	0.5	0	0.8	1.2	3.3
Centre	89.4	3	0.1	5.2	0	0.7	1.5	2.4
Chester	85.5	6.1	0.2	3.9	0	2.4	1.8	6.5
Clarion	97.2	1.2	0.1	0.5	0	0.1	0.8	0.6
Clearfield	95.4	2.3	0.1	0.5	0	0.8	0.9	2.3
Clinton	96.5	1.6	0.1	0.5	0	0.4	0.8	1.1
Columbia	95.4	1.9	0.1	0.8	0	0.7	1.1	2
Crawford	96.3	1.7	0.2	0.5	0	0.2	1.1	0.9
Cumberland	90.9	3.2	0.2	3	0	0.9	1.8	2.7
Dauphin	72.7	18	0.2	3.2	0	2.7	3.1	7
Delaware	72.5	19.7	0.2	4.7	0	0.9	2	3
Elk	98.5	0.3	0.1	0.3	0	0.1	0.7	0.6
Erie	88.2	7.2	0.2	1.1	0	1.2	2.1	3.4
Fayette	93.3	4.6	0.1	0.3	0	0.3	1.3	0.8
Forest	76.9	18	0.2	0.2	0	4.1	0.6	5.4
Franklin	92	3.1	0.2	0.9	0	1.9	1.8	4.3

(Continued)

Table 1.5 (*Continued*)

COUNTY	WHITE	BLACK OR AFRICAN AMERICAN	AMERICAN INDIAN & ALASKA NATIVE	ASIAN	NATIVE HAWAIIAN & OTHER PACIFIC ISLANDER	SOME OTHER RACE	TWO OR MORE RACES	HISPANIC OR LATINO
Fulton	97.3	1	0.2	0.1	0	0.3	1	0.8
Greene	94.6	3.3	0.2	0.3	0	0.7	1	1.2
Huntingdon	92.5	5.2	0.1	0.4	0	0.9	0.9	1.6
Indiana	94.9	2.7	0.1	0.9	0	0.4	0.9	1.1
Jefferson	98.3	0.3	0.2	0.2	0	0.1	0.8	0.6
Juniata	96.8	0.6	0.1	0.3	0	1.1	1	2.5
Lackawanna	92	2.5	0.2	1.7	0	2	1.5	5
Lancaster	88.6	3.7	0.2	1.9	0	3.6	2	8.6
Lawrence	93.8	3.8	0.1	0.4	0	0.2	1.6	1
Lebanon	91	2.2	0.2	1.1	0	3.9	1.6	9.3
Lehigh	79.1	6.1	0.4	2.9	0	8.6	2.9	18.8
Luzerne	90.7	3.4	0.2	1	0	3.3	1.5	6.7
Lycoming	92.6	4.5	0.2	0.6	0	0.4	1.7	1.3
McKean	95.9	2.4	0.2	0.4	0	0.1	0.9	1.7
Mercer	91.6	5.8	0.1	0.6	0	0.3	1.5	1.1
Mifflin	97.5	0.6	0.1	0.4	0	0.3	1	1.1
Monroe	77.2	13.2	0.3	2.1	0	4.3	2.9	13.1
Montgomery	81.1	8.7	0.1	6.4	0	1.6	1.9	4.3
Montour	95.3	1.4	0.1	1.8	0	0.5	1	1.8
Northampton	86.3	5	0.2	2.4	0	3.8	2.2	10.5
Northumberland	95.4	2	0.2	0.4	0	1	1	2.4
Perry	97.4	0.6	0.2	0.4	0	0.4	1	1.3
Philadelphia	41	43.4	0.5	6.3	0	5.9	2.8	12.3
Pike	88.6	5.8	0.3	1	0	2.1	2.1	9
Potter	98.1	0.4	0.3	0.3	0	0.2	0.8	1
Schuylkill	94.4	2.7	0.1	0.5	0	1.3	1	2.8
Snyder	96.9	1.1	0.1	0.5	0	0.5	0.8	1.7
Somerset	96	2.4	0.1	0.3	0	0.6	0.6	1.1

Table 1.5 (*Continued*)

COUNTY	WHITE	BLACK OR AFRICAN AMERICAN	AMERICAN INDIAN & ALASKA NATIVE	ASIAN	NATIVE HAWAIIAN & OTHER PACIFIC ISLANDER	SOME OTHER RACE	TWO OR MORE RACES	HISPANIC OR LATINO
Sullivan	95.9	2.6	0.4	0.3	0	0.1	0.7	1.4
Susquehanna	98	0.4	0.1	0.3	0	0.3	0.8	1.3
Tioga	97.3	0.8	0.2	0.4	0	0.2	1	1
Union	87.7	7.4	0.4	1.2	0.1	1.8	1.6	5.2
Venango	97.1	1	0.2	0.4	0	0.2	1.1	0.9
Warren	98.1	0.4	0.2	0.4	0	0.1	0.8	0.7
Washington	94.1	3.3	0.1	0.6	0	0.3	1.5	1.1
Wayne	94.2	3.1	0.2	0.5	0	0.9	1.1	3.4
Westmoreland	95.3	2.3	0.1	0.7	0	0.2	1.2	0.9

US Department of Census. 2010.

ETHNICITY

A century ago, led by a booming manufacturing economy, Pennsylvania was the epitome of America's melting pot, drawing immigrants from all across the globe seeking to advance their plight. That is not quite the case today. Although the number of foreign-born US residents (naturalized citizens as well as noncitizens who are here legally or illegally) has quadrupled from 9.7 million to 39.9 million in the last fifty years, Pennsylvania's share has largely remained steady, just like its overall population, increasing from 603,000 to 739,000. Nevertheless, the last two decades have seen an actual reversal from the precipitous decline previously experienced in the 1970s and 1980s. In 1990, only 369,000 foreign-born residents resided in the state. Foreign-born residents accounted for 5.3 percent of the state's population in 1960, just slightly below the national average of 5.4 percent. In 2010, however, the percentage was down to 4.1 percent in Pennsylvania, compared to 11.1 percent nationally.[7] Another trend regarding immigration in the state has been the change in the country of origin of these newly arrived immigrants. Prior to 1960, foreign-born residents tended to claim Italy, Germany, Poland, Ireland, or Russia (Soviet Union) as their native homes, whereas today's immigrants are much more likely to be of Hispanic or Asian descent (Table 1.6).

Although immigration trends have shifted over the past several decades, German is still the dominant primary ancestral claim of Pennsylvania's citizens. Slightly over 3.5 million cite it as their primary ancestral home (Table 1.7). This is just over 28 percent of the population as a whole. Those of German ancestry also constitute a plurality in all but four of the state's sixty-seven counties, with the exceptions being Delaware and Lackawanna (Irish), Philadelphia

Table 1.6 Foreign-Born Population by Country of Origin, 2010

REGION	POPULATION
Europe	183,693
Asia	282,035
Africa	52,071
Latin America	221,269
Total	739,068

US Department of Census. 2010.

Table 1.7 Ancestry

TOTAL POPULATION	12,702,379	100%
American	539,348	4.30%
Arab	60,595	0.50%
Czech	57,694	0.50%
Danish	19,137	0.20%
Dutch	275,149	2.20%
English	105,837	8.50%
French	234,589	1.90%
French Canadian	30,884	0.20%
German	3,544,820	28.50%
Greek	65,755	0.50%
Hungarian	146,502	1.20%
Irish	2,259,060	18.20%
Italian	1,588,990	12.80%
Lithuanian	83,373	0.70%
Norwegian	41,572	0.30%
Polish	890,440	7.20%
Portuguese	18,680	0.20%
Russian	202,069	1.60%
Scotch-Irish	252,684	2.00%
Scottish	212,780	1.70%

(Continued)

Table 1.7 (*Continued*)

TOTAL POPULATION	12,702,379	100%
Slovak	248,478	2.00%
Sub-Saharan African	77,201	0.60%
Swedish	117,709	0.90%
Swiss	72,008	0.60%
Ukrainian	121,590	1.00%
Welsh	188,430	1.50%
West Indian	58,423	0.50%

US Department of Census. 2010.

(African Americans), and Luzerne (Polish). The second-largest category includes those of Irish background, who number over 2.2 million and make up 18.2 percent of the population. Individuals who claimed Italian ancestry registered third with over 1.5 million (12.8 percent). The number of African Americans residing in the state is just shy of 1.5 million, as previously mentioned, although those who cite this category as their primary ancestry is only 9.6 percent, less than the number cited earlier due to the exclusion here of those who identify as mixed race, a separate category according to the US Census. Pennsylvanians of English background come in fifth at just over one million (8.5 percent), while those of Polish extraction fall in sixth place with just slightly below 900,000 residents, or 7.2 percent of the population. Finally, as also noted above, the overall Hispanic (though here all Hispanics are grouped together) population in Pennsylvania is over 789,000, slightly over 6 percent of the state.

RELIGION

Estimates of Pennsylvanians' religious backgrounds suggest that approximately 73 percent of the state's population adhere to some recognized faith, which is less than the national average of 77 percent. This ranks the commonwealth tied for thirty-fourth overall in the percentage of worshipers.[8]

Among various denominations, 19 percent categorize themselves as Evangelical Christian, less than the national average of 25 percent, ranking it in thirty-eight position among all states. However, among states in the Northeast, Pennsylvania tops the list in first place, where the overall average in the region is just 13 percent. Since 2007, the last time this information was compiled, the share of the Evangelical population has increased one percent (Table 1.8).

The proportion of mainline Protestants in Pennsylvania is 23 percent, considerably higher than the national average of 14 percent. This places the state eighth nationally and highest in the Northeast, though it is a two-point drop since 2007. Historically black Protestant churches

Table 1.8 Religious Composition of Pennsylvania

DENOMINATION	PERCENT
Christian	73%
Catholic	24%
Mainline Protestant	23%
Evangelical Protestant	19%
Historically Black Protestant	5%
Jehovah's Witness	1%
Mormon	<1%
Orthodox Christian	<1%
Other Christian	<1%
Non-Christian Faiths	6%
Jewish	1%
Muslim	1%
Hindu	1%
Buddhist	<1%
Other World Religions	<1%
Other Faiths	2%
Unaffiliated (religious "nones")	21%
Agnostic	4%
Atheist	3%
Nothing in Particular	14%
Don't Know	1%

Source: Pew Research Center.

maintain five percent of the state's population, one point less than the average across the nation, which places it in a tie for thirty-fourth with six others. The 5 percent also constitutes a two-point drop during the same time frame.

Pennsylvania's Catholic population presents perhaps the biggest shift in the last few years. The overall number is now 24 percent, a five-point decline from just a few years ago. Nationally, the share of identified Catholics has also declined, though less precipitously, from 24 to 21 percent. This decline is also shared by other states in the Northeast, where the number has slipped even more noticeably from 37 to 30 percent overall. The number of Catholics in the state is below most in the Northeast, containing less than all states but Maine and Vermont. Compared to all fifty states, the Catholic population ranks fourteenth overall.

It should be noted that the number of unaffiliated voters in Pennsylvania has risen considerably in recent years, from 13 to 21 percent. This reflects the shift that has occurred nationally, where those not claiming a religious adherence rose from 16 to 23 percent during that time. The percentage of unaffiliated residents in Pennsylvania places the state thirty-fourth overall nationally.

AGE

Over the past sixty years, Pennsylvania's median age has increased from thirty-two to 40.1 (Table 1.9). This places the state well above the national average of 36.8 and sixth nationally, behind Maine, Vermont, West Virginia, New Hampshire, and Florida, respectively. In 1960,

Table 1.9 Ranking of States by Highest Median Age

RANK	MEDIAN AGE	STATE	POPULATION
1.	42.70	Maine	1,328,361
2.	41.50	Vermont	625,741
3.	41.30	West Virginia	1,852,994
4.	41.10	New Hampshire	1,316,470
5.	40.70	Florida	18,801,310
6.	40.10	Pennsylvania	12,702,379
7.	40.00	Connecticut	3,574,097
8.	39.80	Montana	989,415
9.	39.40	Rhode Island	1,052,567
10.	39.10	Massachusetts	6,547,629
11.	39.00	New Jersey	8,791,894
12.	38.90	Michigan	9,883,640
13.	38.80	Ohio	11,536,504
13.	38.80	Delaware	897,934
15.	38.60	Hawaii	1,360,301
16.	38.50	Wisconsin	5,686,986
17.	38.40	Oregon	3,831,074
18.	38.10	Kentucky	4,339,367
18.	38.10	Iowa	3,046,355
20.	38.00	New York	19,378,102
20.	38.00	Maryland	5,773,552
20.	38.00	Tennessee	6,346,105

(Continued)

Table 1.9 (*Continued*)

RANK	MEDIAN AGE	STATE	POPULATION
23.	37.90	South Carolina	4,625,364
23.	37.90	Missouri	5,988,927
23.	37.90	Alabama	4,779,736
26.	37.50	Virginia	8,001,024
27.	37.40	North Carolina	9,535,483
27.	37.40	Arkansas	2,915,918
27.	37.40	Minnesota	5,303,925
30.	37.30	Washington	6,724,540
31.	37.00	North Dakota	672,591
31.	37.00	Indiana	6,483,802
33.	36.90	South Dakota	814,180
34.	36.80	Wyoming	563,626
35.	36.70	New Mexico	2,059,179
36.	36.60	Illinois	12,830,632
37.	36.30	Nevada	2,700,551
38.	36.20	Oklahoma	3,751,351
38.	36.20	Nebraska	1,826,341
40.	36.10	Colorado	5,029,196
41.	36.00	Kansas	2,853,118
41.	36.00	Mississippi	2,967,297
43.	35.90	Arizona	6,392,017
44.	35.80	Louisiana	4,533,372
45.	35.30	Georgia	9,687,653
46.	35.20	California	37,253,956
47.	34.60	Idaho	1,567,582
48.	33.80	Alaska	710,231
48.	33.80	District of Columbia	601,723
50.	33.60	Texas	25,145,561
51.	29.20	Utah	2,763,885

Source: US Department of Census. 2010.

only 9.9 percent of the state's population was over sixty-five. In 2010, the number increased to 16.7 percent, above the national average of 14.5 percent. This growth of the older population in Pennsylvania and the United States as a whole impacts a myriad of areas, including education, housing, the labor force, and, of course, health care, just to name a few. As the aging of the state and nation continues, with estimates predicting the percentage of adults sixty-five and older reaching as high as 20 percent, the impact that an aging population presents will only increase, posing a considerable problem for future policymakers.

EDUCATION

Unlike most industrialized countries, the United States does not have a national ministry of education with sole control over education. Although the Department of Education was created in 1978 during the Carter Administration, its authority has been limited and its support rather tepid in some quarters. Many politicians, particularly conservatives, have campaigned on a pledge to eliminate it, arguing that the Tenth Amendment gives the states sole responsibility for any power not granted specifically to the national government. Thus, despite efforts of the federal government to impose a greater degree of accountability through efforts such as No Child Left Behind, education across the nation is still largely a matter for the states and (in most cases) local school boards.

Although not as specifically detailed on the subject as many other states', Pennsylvania's constitution does clearly spell out that "the General Assembly shall provide for the maintenance and support of a thorough and efficient system of public education to serve the needs of the Commonwealth." This has been legally defined under state law to mandate school attendance for a child between the ages of eight and seventeen or until graduation from high school. For fiscal year 2013–14, the state spent $13,864 per pupil, above the national average of $10,700.[9] The overall expenditure for K–12 education at the state level is now approaching $6 billion annually.

Pennsylvania ranks in the middle of the pack when analyzing the overall results, however. The high school graduation rate of 87.9 percent is just above the national average of 85.3 percent, placing it twenty-fourth nationally. Those obtaining a bachelor's degree tally 26.4 percent of the state, just below the national average of 27.9 percent, which ranks Pennsylvania twenty-sixth nationally, while the 10.2 percent of the state's citizens with an advanced degree mirrors the national average, placing it nineteenth overall in relation to the other fifty states.

While state law outlines the basic rules and regulations governing education policy, local control at the school board level, in most cases, still has the final word regarding both budgetary and policy-related items. For the former, while the state provides considerable assistance, each individual school district is the final arbiter over how much money is spent and how it is allocated. Financial support at the local level is generated primarily through use of the property tax. Regarding policy-related issues, it is, for example, the decision of the school board as to what athletic teams and student organizations are available or whether students should be required to wear school uniforms.

There are currently five hundred independent school districts in the state. Over the years, there has been a debate on whether that number should be shrunk through consolidation;

however, resistance to that has been intense. Debate continues on whether consolidating school districts would actually deliver the reduction in costs that proponents promise. The impact of consolidation on rural schools is especially concerning to many. Also, school districts are the core for many communities' identification, and local citizens are highly reluctant to give that up.

There are also 163 charter schools in Pennsylvania that are funded by the host school district but are independently structurally. These are "brick and mortar" schools whose supporters believe provide a better learning environment than the traditional school. The proliferation of these charters over the past few years, particularly within the city of Philadelphia, has become a major political issue, with some arguing that it provides diversity of education and better meets the needs of selected students, while others claim that, by draining resources and support from the home school district, it contributes to poorer performance for their students. There are also fourteen cyber charter schools in the state that operate under the auspices of the State Department of Education. They have a limited physical plant, with a large part of the teacher-to-student communication being conducted electronically over the Internet. Comparatively speaking, one national proponent of charter initiatives ranks Pennsylvania fourteenth nationally in its support of this alternative-style education.[10]

In addition, there are over two thousand private schools, serving approximately three hundred thousand students, located in the state. Of these, 64 percent are religiously affiliated, primarily Roman Catholic or Christian. However, the Pennsylvania Constitution specifically details that "no money raised for the support of the public schools of the Commonwealth shall be appropriated to or used for the support of any sectarian school." Therefore, these private schools do not receive any financial support directly from the state, though the state is able to provide assistance, as sanctioned by the United States Supreme Court, in such matters as transportation, textbooks, lunches, and, of course, police and fire protection.[11]

Pennsylvania is also home to a rather large number of colleges and universities. There are fourteen institutions in the State System of Higher Education, with a total undergraduate enrollment of slightly over one hundred thousand students. The largest is West Chester University, with over sixteen thousand students. These universities are creatures of the state itself. While they also receive state funding (though they are not owned by the commonwealth), over 130,000 students attend one of the four state-related institutions located within Pennsylvania. These include Lincoln University, a historically black college located in Chester County, as well as Penn State, Temple University, and the University of Pittsburgh, each of which also have created branch campuses throughout the state. Community colleges enroll the largest number of state-affiliated students, at just shy of 150,000. There are fourteen in all, a few of which also have branch campuses. There are also eight institutions organized as private state-aided institutions, the largest of which are Drexel University and the University of Pennsylvania. Over thirty thousand undergraduates attend these colleges, which, while private, do receive financial support from the state. The largest grouping overall, however, is of private colleges and universities in Pennsylvania. Over 180,000 undergraduates, some of whom are religiously based, attend these schools, the largest of which is Carnegie-Mellon, with just under six thousand students. Most, however, enroll under three thousand; the smallest of these is Gratz College, with just under one thousand students. There are also six private two-year colleges in the state (with a total combined enrollment of approximately seven thousand students), sixteen theological seminaries (enrollment unreported), and one college of technology, the Thaddeus Stevens College of Technology, located in Lancaster, which has just under one thousand students.[12]

MEDIA

With almost three million households, Philadelphia boasts the largest of the six media markets located across the state, and it is ranked fourth nationally, behind New York, Los Angeles, and Chicago. It covers eight counties in Pennsylvania, the city itself, the four surrounding suburbs, Berks County, and it reaches into the Lehigh Valley, to Lehigh and Northampton Counties. Additionally, eight counties in middle and southern New Jersey are included as well as two counties in Delaware and one in Maryland.

The second-largest media market in the state is based in Pittsburgh, with over 2.7 million households. It includes twelve counties in the southwestern part of the state as well as two counties from West Virginia and one from Maryland. The number of households served is over 1.1 million, which places it twenty-third nationally. The Harrisburg-Lancaster-Lebanon-York market comes in at third in the state, serving nine counties and approximately seven hundred thousand households in the midstate area. It ranks as the forty-third largest in the United States.

The fourth-largest market, Scranton-Wilkes-Barre, combines sixteen counties stretching across the northeastern and north central sections of the state. The 580,000 households that reside here make it the fifty-fourth largest in the nation. Fifth largest in the state is the Johnstown-Altoona market in the midwestern region of Pennsylvania, with 280,000 households. Encompassing eleven counties in all, it is the 102nd largest in the nation. The smallest media market in the state is based in Erie and contains four counties overall, with a little over 150,000 households.

Four other markets include Pennsylvania counties but are based in a contiguous state. In fact, Wayne County is located in the nation's largest, the New York City market. Sparsely populated Potter County is included in the Buffalo, New York market, the fifty-second largest, while Lawrence and Mercer Counties are located in the Youngstown, Ohio market, which ranks 110th. Finally, on the New York border, Tioga County is located in the Elmira-Corning market, the 174th largest out of the 210 that exist across the nation.[13]

There are currently forty-nine daily newspapers published across the state. Six are included among the top 130 nationally, with the Philadelphia Inquirer at the top, with 325,000 subscribers (placing it sixteenth overall). The Pittsburgh Post-Gazette ranks second with 188,000 subscribers (thirty-seventh), followed by the Philadelphia Daily News, which comes in at seventy-fourth nationally with 110,000 subscribers, and the Allentown Morning Call, which ranks eightieth with 100,000. The last state daily paper that makes the list is the Harrisburg Patriot-News, based in the state capital, with 70,000 subscribers, placing it 115th overall in the country.[14]

Lastly, there are also 557 radio stations licensed by the Federal Communications Commission in the commonwealth, with three broadcasting at the maximum allowable power of 50,000 watts. Those three are 1020 KDKA in Pittsburgh (news/talk), and in Philadelphia, 1060 (news), and 1210 (news/talk).[15]

ECONOMY

Without question, Pennsylvania is still one of the nation's industrial leaders. Its gross domestic product in 2014 of $644 billion places the state sixth in the nation, the same ranking as its overall population in relation to the other states.[16] However, its role has diminished considerably since the early twentieth century, when, spurred by oil and coal production in the west, it was the country's leading energy producer. The US steel industry was also centered in the state, with Pittsburgh-based US Steel and Bethlehem-based Bethlehem Steel leading the way. While munitions production during World War II, along with significant federally aided stimulus programs, spurred a bit of a rebound during the 1940s and 1950s, some sections of the state have never fully recovered from the damage of the Depression years.

The decline continued in the decades that followed but then accelerated in the early 1980s, when pressures from both foreign competition and a national economic recession devastated entire regions of the state. From 1979 to 1985, Pennsylvania lost over 21 percent of its manufacturing jobs while unemployment hit a high of 14.9 percent.[17] In addition, throughout the decade of the 1980s, the state witnessed declines in other areas as well. Manufacturers of construction equipment lost twelve thousand workers, the general industrial machinery sector declined by eight thousand, and employment in the metalwork machinery industry declined by seven thousand. Makers of women's and misses' outerwear lost twenty-five thousand jobs, knitting mills nine thousand, and manufacturers of men's and boys' furnishings more than seven thousand.[18]

While Pennsylvania's manufacturing base has eroded from its storied past, some of the loss has been offset by job gains in other areas in more recent years. The service sector has now become the state's leading source of employment, with over five million people employed (Table 1.10). The most robust growth in the service-sector industry has been in the medical or health-related fields, which include hospitals, nursing and personal care facilities, residential care, and home health care services. Other service-sector employers, such as industries serving businesses or providing consumers with non-health-related services, have also shown resiliency. Financial services such as the insurance sector (including health and non-health-related concerns), real

Table 1.10 Current Employment Statistics for Pennsylvania

INDUSTRY	NUMBER EMPLOYED
Total Nonfarm	5,855,700
Total Private	5,141,500
Goods-Producing	841,800
Service-Providing	5,013,900
Private-Service-Providing	4,299,700
Mining and Logging	35,500
Construction	241,400
Manufacturing	564,900
Durable Goods	340,000
Nondurable Goods	224,900
Trade, Transportation, and Utilities	1,127,700
Wholesale Trade	228,700
Retail Trade	636,900
Transportation and Utilities	262,100
Information	86,400
Financial Activities	320,300
Finance and insurance	258,500
Real Estate and Rental and Leasing	61,800
Professional and Business Services	765,600
Professional, Scientific, and Technical Services	340,300
Management of Companies and Enterprises	133,000
Administrative and Support and Waste Management and Remediation Services	292,300
Education and Health Services	1,201,800
Educational Services	237,500
Health Care and Social Assistance	964,300
Leisure and Hospitality	543,800
Arts, Entertainment, and Recreation	95,200
Accommodation and Food services	448,600
Other Services	254,100
Government	714,200
Federal Government	95,500
State Government	158,300
Local Government	460,400

Source: PA Department of Labor and Industry. August 2015.

estate, and commercial banks, have also continued to do well. Represented by eating and drinking establishments, grocery stores, and drug stores, the retail-trade sector has also been strong. Finally, other areas that have produced consistent growth over the past several years have been legal services, colleges and universities, and amusement and recreational services.

Like the rest of the nation, Pennsylvania began the decade of the 1970s with a solid economy, with unemployment rates at just 3.2 percent in the state, considerably lower than the national average of 3.9 percent (Table 1.11). Neither set has been duplicated since. Unemployment

Table 1.11 Unemployment Rate in Pennsylvania As Compared with National Rate

YEAR	PA	US
1970	3.2%	3.9%
1971	5.1%	5.9%
1972	5.9%	5.8%
1973	3.9%	4.9%
1974	4.7%	5.1%
1975	7.8%	8.1%
1976	8.0%	7.9%
1977	8.0%	7.5%
1978	7.3%	6.4%
1979	6.8%	5.9%
1980	7.1%	6.3%
1981	7.9%	7.5%
1982	9.9%	8.6%
1983	12.0%	10.4%
1984	9.7%	8.0%
1985	8.4%	7.3%
1986	7.5%	6.7%
1987	5.9%	6.6%
1988	5.4%	5.7%
1989	4.6%	5.4%
1990	5.1%	5.4%
1991	6.6%	6.4%
1992	7.6%	7.3%
1993	7.2%	7.3%
1994	6.6%	6.6%

(Continued)

Table 1.11 (*Continued*)

YEAR	PA	US
1995	5.8%	5.6%
1996	5.9%	5.6%
1997	5.3%	5.3%
1998	4.7%	4.6%
1999	4.5%	4.3%
2000	4.1%	4.0%
2001	4.3%	4.2%
2002	5.6%	5.7%
2003	5.8%	5.8%
2004	5.5%	5.7%
2005	5.2%	5.3%
2006	4.6%	4.7%
2007	4.3%	4.6%
2008	4.8%	5.0%
2009	7.2%	7.8%
2010	8.6%	9.8%
2011	7.9%	9.2%
2012	7.6%	8.3%
2013	7.6%	8.0%
2014	6.3%	6.6%
2015	5.1%	5.7%
2016	4.9%	4.6%

Source: PA Department of Labor and Industry.

continued to increase throughout this stagnant decade until the recession of the early 1980s cratered the economies of both the state and the nation. In January 1983, the state reached its highest level of unemployment since the Great Depression at 12 percent, almost two percentage points higher than the national average.

Since that time, however, the state's economy has rebounded and largely kept ahead of the national average. In the twenty-nine years that elapsed between January 1987 and January 2015, Pennsylvania's unemployment rate was below the national average in all but eight (two were tied). In fact, this has been the case in every year since 2002. The most recent unemployment statistics at the time of publication is 4.6 percent in Pennsylvania, compared to 4.9 percent nationally (for all other years, the benchmark used was the month of January).

Unemployment rates throughout the commonwealth also vary considerably, as Table 1.12 demonstrates. Counties with the highest rates of unemployment tend to be concentrated in the

Table 1.12 Ranking of Unemployed in Pennsylvania Counties

RANK	AREA	UNEMPLOYMENT RATE
1	Forest County	7.6%
2	Fayette County	7.3%
3	Potter County	6.9%
4	Venango County	6.8%
5	Cameron County	6.7%
6	Monroe County	6.7%
7	Somerset County	6.5%
8	Armstrong County	6.4%
9	Clearfield County	6.4%
10	Greene County	6.3%
11	Huntingdon County	6.3%
12	Philadelphia County	6.3%
13	McKean County	6.1%
14	Tioga County	6.1%
15	Cambria County	6.0%
16	Indiana County	6.0%
17	Jefferson County	6.0%
18	Northumberland	6.0%
19	Pike County	6.0%
20	Lawrence County	5.9%
21	Clinton County	5.7%
22	Luzerne County	5.7%
23	Schuylkill County	5.7%
24	Carbon County	5.6%
25	Lycoming County	5.6%
26	Fulton County	5.5%
27	Clarion County	5.5%
28	Washington County	5.5%
29	Bedford County	5.4%
30	Beaver County	5.7%
31	Mercer County	5.5%
32	Elk County	5.4%
33	Bradford County	5.3%
34	Sullivan County	5.3%

(*Continued*)

Table 1.12 (*Continued*)

RANK	AREA	UNEMPLOYMENT RATE
35	Wyoming County	5.3%
36	Crawford County	5.5%
37	Erie County	5.9%
38	Wayne County	5.2%
39	Westmoreland County	5.2%
40	Mifflin County	5.1%
41	Lackawanna County	5.0%
42	Lehigh County	5.0%
43	Warren County	5.0%
44	Juniata County	4.9%
45	Allegheny County	4.8%
46	Blair County	4.8%
47	Northampton County	4.8%
48	Susquehanna County	4.8%
49	Columbia County	4.6%
50	Franklin County	4.6%
51	Berks County	4.5%
52	Delaware County	4.5%
53	Butler County	4.5%
54	Snyder County	4.5%
55	Dauphin County	4.4%
56	Union County	4.4%
57	Bucks County	4.3%
58	Lebanon County	4.1%
59	Perry County	4.1%
60	York County	4.1%
61	Lancaster County	3.8%
62	Montgomery County	3.8%
63	Cumberland County	3.7%
64	Montour County	3.7%
65	Adams County	3.6%
66	Centre County	3.5%
67	Chester County	3.5%

Source: PA Department of Labor and Industry.

western or northern-tier parts of the state. Forest County, the third smallest in the state, possesses the highest rate of unemployment at 7.6 percent. In fact, of the twenty counties with the highest unemployment rates in the state, only three fall outside these two areas: Philadelphia (fourth), Monroe (tenth), and Luzerne (thirteenth). At the other end of the spectrum, Chester County, located in the southeast, and Centre County (home of Penn State University), in the middle of the state, benefit from having the lowest levels, with just 3.8 percent of the workforce unemployed.

Table 1.12 shows the counties in Pennsylvania with the highest monthly seasonally adjusted unemployment rate in July 2015.

AGRICULTURE

The most noticeable development in Pennsylvania's agricultural sector over the past half century has been the number of farms in operation. In 1960, there were slightly over a hundred thousand farms, compared with only a little over 59,300 listed in 2012. Small, family-sized farms still predominate; the average size of farms is only 130 acres, far below the national average of 434 acres. Only 139 farms across the state cover are of over two thousand acres. Overall, Pennsylvania ranks nineteenth out of the fifty states nationally in the total value of its produce.

Almost 70 percent of Pennsylvania's agricultural income is generated by livestock and livestock products, with milk being the most important product in this category. In the northern region of the state, dairy products—chickens and eggs—are the leading source of farm income and the most important product. Beef and cattle rank second and are produced in particularly high numbers in Bradford, Greene, York, Washington, and Lancaster Counties. In crop production, greenhouse and nursery products generate the most revenue, while mushrooms, largely grown in Chester and Delaware Counties (the top national producers of mushrooms), rank second statewide. The state also ranks second in apple production while also being a large producer of grapes, peaches, and strawberries. Vegetables also contribute to the state's agricultural economy, particularly sweet corn, potatoes, tomatoes, beans, and cabbage. In addition, corn for grain, hay, and soybean crops are important to the state's agricultural economy, as are other field crops grown in the state: wheat, tobacco, and oats. Lastly, it should be noted that Pennsylvania ranks third overall nationally in the production of organic food products.[19]

TAXATION

The two largest sources of state revenue in Pennsylvania are income taxes on individuals and businesses and the state sales tax. In addition, the state imposes other taxes and fees on businesses and collects fees for various licenses and permits. There is also an inheritance tax; taxes on gasoline, diesel fuel, alcoholic beverages, and tobacco; taxes and fees on certain other goods and services; and a tax on the transfer of real property. Pennsylvania is one of only five

American states to employ a flat tax on personal income, at 3.07 percent. Unlike the many other states, Pennsylvania has a pure flat tax, pursuant to the state constitution, with no personal exemptions.

The state also assesses a 6 percent sales tax on taxable goods and services. Counties may also add additional sales tax charges, but only Philadelphia and Allegheny have opted to institute this increase. There is also a multitude of exempted items, such as unprepared food (not ready-to-eat), most clothing, shoes, drugs, textbooks, and residential heating fuels. Pennsylvania does not levy or collect taxes on real estate or personal property, though counties, municipalities, and school districts do levy taxes on real estate. In addition, some local municipalities such as Philadelphia assess a wage tax on personal income. Generally, the total wage tax rate is capped at 1 percent of income, but some municipalities with home rule charters may charge more than that amount. While comparing taxes imposed in one state with others is difficult due to the complexity of various formulas used across the country, Pennsylvania generally falls just outside the top ten states that have the highest tax burdens in the nation.

2 POLITICAL PARTIES AND ELECTIONS IN PENNSYLVANIA

POLITICAL REALIGNMENT

When assessing the development of American political parties throughout the nation's history, political historians tend to think in terms of partisan realignments. Basically, a realigning election is one that is so monumental that much of what previously occurred has now been upended. It is an election in which such sudden and dramatic change takes place that the coalitions that divide the two parties and the issues that dominate them have been transformed virtually overnight.

In terms of national politics, the consensus of most scholars is that we've witnessed six party systems throughout our history. The initial party system began as a result of a conflict between the Federalist Party and their Democratic-Republican opponents (led by Thomas Jefferson), who differed on the role of the national government in the burgeoning democracy. Their opposition to the War of 1812 sealed the fate of the pro-British Federalists, who had been in decline since President Adams was defeated by Jefferson in the presidential election of 1800. During this time, the Federalist Party found little support in Pennsylvania, as the state voted for Democratic-Republicans even in 1796, the last presidential election won by the Federalists. For a little over a decade, the Democratic-Republicans were the only major party, the sole instance of one-party rule in our nation's history.

After President Andrew Jackson's victory in the 1828 election, the Democratic-Republicans split into several different factions, the most prominent of which was the Democratic Party, the label adopted by Jackson's supporters. At the center of their political philosophy rested the idea that the powers of the national government should be curtailed while giving more authority for domestic governing to the states. While Pennsylvania was a strong supporter of Jackson's views, elsewhere there emerged a coalition of elites, native-born Protestants, and reformers who strongly objected to his anti-Washington attacks.

They were led by congressional leaders such as John Quincy Adams, Henry Clay, and Daniel Webster, who ultimately split to form an alternate party, the Whigs. Table 2.1 outlines the various political party systems in both United States and Pennsylvania history.

Table 2.1 Party System in United States and Pennsylvania History

PARTY SYSTEM	YEARS	DESCRIPTION	YEARS	DESCRIPTION
First Party System	1789–1836	Jeffersonians Dominant	1789–1836	Jeffersonians Dominant
Second Party System	1836–1860	Democrats v. Whigs	1836–1860	Democrats Dominant
Third Party System	1860–1896	Two-Party Competitive	1860–1954	Republican Dominant
Fourth Party System	1896–1932	Republican Dominant	1954–1992	Two-Party Competitive
Fifth Party System	1932–1968	Democratic Dominant	1992–Present	Two-Party Competitive With Intrastate Realignment
Sixth Party System	1968–Present	Divided Government		

Decades later, the issue of slavery ultimately crushed the Democratic Party in Pennsylvania. Ironically, it was Pennsylvania's only US president, James Buchanan—who was ambivalent on the issue and idled as the Southern states seceded—which contributed to the party's downfall in the state. In 1856, a new abolitionist party (called the Republican Party) was formed and held its first convention in Pittsburgh that year. Four years later, with the Whig Party splintered as well over slavery, the election of Republican Abraham Lincoln and the coming Civil War would change the course of parties in Pennsylvania. Few states were as impacted by the war, and certainly fewer in the North, as it was on Pennsylvania's soil that the tide of the Confederacy reached its height and ultimately crested on the battlefields outside the town of Gettysburg.

Radical Republicans such as Pennsylvania's Thaddeus Stevens supported harsh conditions on the South. This certainly satisfied many Pennsylvanians, as the Democratic Party came to represent appeasement toward the South among many in the state. In addition, the GOP's strong support of the high tariff sat well with the manufacturing interests of the commonwealth, while the Democrats adopted a low-tariff philosophy, which was more popular in the Southern states. The third party system also witnessed the pinnacle of the dominant urban political party machine, of which the Pennsylvania Republican Party stood as a prime example. Bosses like Simon Cameron, Matthew Quay, and Boies Penrose would lead the GOP not simply to prominence but to dominance during this period of time.

Nationally, the fourth party system was a period of Republican rule that began in the aftermath of Williams Jennings Bryan's nomination for president as the Democratic Party's standard bearer in 1896. Bryan's populist, anti-immigrant, and anti-urban worker message wiped out much of whatever support his party had in other states north of the Mason-Dixon Line. For Pennsylvania, however, already controlled by the GOP, it only exacerbated the dire situation that befell the Democrats in this state. At the turn of the twentieth century, the political battle in the state wasn't one between Republicans and Democrats but rather between conservative and progressive Republicans.

The stock market crash of 1929 would, however, reverse the fortunes of the two major parties nationwide, and three years later, the nation would elect Franklin D. Roosevelt. Roosevelt's more aggressive economic initiatives and leadership during World War II would help create the New Deal coalition nationally. This alliance of northern urbanites, Southerners, Catholics, Jews, and African Americans would comprise the most dominant political coalition of the twentieth century. However, as one of only six states carried by Republican President Herbert Hoover, Pennsylvania was slow to respond to its call. Still, as Roosevelt's agenda unfolded, Pittsburgh, like most other northern cities, eventually fell to the Democrats, which led them to victory two years later in the gubernatorial election of 1934, only the second time since the Civil War that had occurred. And while Roosevelt was able to carry the state in his 1936 landslide, the GOP regained control of Pennsylvania two years later in the next election for governor. The foremost reason for their continued political hegemony in the state was their continued control of Pennsylvania's biggest prize, the city of Philadelphia, which remained in the dominion of the tight grip of the local GOP machine. Essentially, the state remained locked in its own third party system.

That would finally come to an end, however, when the sort of corruption that tends to solidify after a century of virtually unchallenged supremacy contributed to its demise. This ensued after a group of reformers, led by mayoral candidate Joe Clark, finally seized control of Philadelphia's City Hall in 1951 for the Democrats, and they've held onto it ever since. Three years later, another machine reformer, George Leader, captured the governorship, and with that, the state finally welcomed a legitimate two-party system within its borders. For the next several decades that followed, the two parties found themselves locked in a tight competitive balance. From 1952–1988, Pennsylvania's presidential vote mirrored the national one with only one exception, when it went for Democrat Hubert Humphrey over Richard Nixon in 1968.

Reflecting this tight competition between the two major parties, a fascinating pattern also developed in the 1950s in which control of the governor's mansion would rotate every eight years until it was finally broken in the most recent election in 2014. In the other major statewide contests, while the GOP was dominant in elections for the United States Senate, this was usually the result of benefiting from internecine Democratic Party feuds or simply possessing more appealing candidates than anything else. Control of the state's congressional delegation and the state legislature were also closely matched. As for registration, the Democrats would eventually overtake the Republicans in the early 1970s and continue to hold a narrow advantage throughout the remainder of the state's fourth party system.

Nationally, the fifth party system is now considered by most scholars to have begun with the election of President Richard Nixon in 1968, an election in which highly salient issues such as the Vietnam War and civil rights shattered the long-standing New Deal coalition. However, unlike previous realignments throughout our nation's history, the Republican Party did not awaken the day after this election as the country's new majority party. Rather than a realignment occurring, this new system produced what would become known as a dealigning electorate. Generally speaking, a dealigning electorate is delineated by a movement away from both political parties. This is manifested in a variety of ways, such as an increase in Independent identifiers, the growth of candidate-centered campaigns (rather than party focused), and voters more willing to split their ticket. Divided government, with one party controlling the White House and the other Congress, would serve as the norm in the decades to follow. Beginning in 1968, for only a little over fourteen years did we have true one-party control: eight for the Democrats and a little over six for the Republicans (the GOP held the Senate for only a few months in 2001 prior to the defection of Vermont senator Jim Jeffords, whose move threw control to the Democrats).

Likewise, the fifth party system in Pennsylvania, which began in 1992, has also taken on a different tone. Not dramatic, like the national realignment of 1968, it has been somewhat difficult to even notice while it has been unfolding. However, there is little question that significant change is underway in the state. Essentially, what we are now witnessing in Pennsylvania is the development of a bifurcated state. At the macro level, the Democrats appear to have the upper hand, with almost one million more registered voters, victories in six of the last seven (though not the most recent) presidential contests, and a developing advantage in the other elections contested statewide. However, at the micro level, where legislative districts are either drawn or historically marked, the Republicans are more likely to prevail; this is demonstrated currently by the party holding an overwhelming majority of the state's delegation in the United States House of Representatives, both houses of the state legislature, and the vast majority of the county governments across the state.

More than anything, the source for this is the development of a geographical realignment that has occurred throughout many parts of the state. In fact, Pennsylvania is increasingly becoming a tale of two states, each one going in different directions. In the southeast suburbs of Philadelphia, which the Republicans depended on to offset losses experienced within the city itself, Democratic voter registration has surged in the past decade, leading them to now outnumber their rivals in this four-county region. However, the cultural issues that have largely contributed to the creation of this Democratic majority in the southeastern suburbs—issues such as same-sex marriage, abortion, and gun control—have not occurred within a vacuum. They have largely been responsible for another, though not as sharply noted, realignment happening elsewhere in the state, and in particular the southwest. In the counties surrounding Pittsburgh, the base of the Democratic Party since 1932, voters are more and more rejecting their traditional allegiances and gravitating to the Republicans. The section that follows will attempt to illustrate how these shifting allegiances ultimately play out and will determine which party (if any) will control the immediate future in Pennsylvania politics.

PARTY REGISTRATION IN PENNSYLVANIA

Based upon data provided by the Pennsylvania Department of State, at the time of the 2016 general election, the Democratic Party, with just over 4.2 million registered voters, fell just shy of an absolute majority but had a clear plurality with 48.3 percent of all registered voters—almost a ten-point advantage over their Republican rivals (Table 2.2) This amounts to an advantage of slightly over 916,000 registered voters. Those who registered as Other Party tallied over 1.2 million, or 13.8 percent overall.

Table 2.2 Voter Registration in Pennsylvania, January 2017

COUNTY	DEM	PERCENT	REP	PERCENT	OTHER	PERCENT	TOTAL
Adams	19,197	29.8%	35,266	54.7%	6,273	9.7%	64,526
Allegheny	538,966	58.3%	260,063	28.1%	73,612	8.0%	925,151
Armstrong	15,038	36.5%	21,721	52.7%	2,393	5.8%	41,228
Beaver	56,185	51.6%	39,772	36.5%	6,168	5.7%	108,905
Bedford	8,148	26.4%	19,951	64.6%	1,545	5.0%	30,883
Berks	113,681	45.8%	97,914	39.4%	22,970	9.3%	248,212
Blair	22,868	30.3%	43,420	57.6%	5,117	6.8%	75,348
Bradford	9,846	27.3%	21,651	60.1%	2,305	6.4%	36,002
Bucks	195,141	42.9%	186,782	41.0%	43,044	9.5%	455,307
Butler	39,826	32.0%	67,726	54.5%	9,466	7.6%	124,311
Cambria	42,808	51.6%	31,967	38.5%	5,679	6.8%	82,993
Cameron	1,202	37.2%	1,658	51.3%	192	5.9%	3,234
Carbon	18,229	43.3%	17,699	42.0%	3,375	8.0%	42,120
Centre	51,115	41.4%	47,635	38.6%	17,605	14.3%	123,358
Chester	131,836	38.4%	151,827	44.2%	31,469	9.2%	343,213
Clarion	7,622	33.4%	12,694	55.6%	1,581	6.9%	22,818
Clearfield	20,137	38.6%	25,936	49.7%	2,878	5.5%	52,159
Clinton	9,098	40.8%	10,225	45.9%	1,818	8.2%	22,292
Columbia	14,992	39.0%	17,676	46.0%	3,690	9.6%	38,441
Crawford	19,296	36.2%	27,618	51.8%	3,642	6.8%	53,270
Cumberland	55,388	33.3%	85,179	51.1%	16,130	9.7%	166,533
Dauphin	82,211	45.2%	74,599	41.0%	15,184	8.3%	182,048

(Continued)

Table 2.2 (*Continued*)

COUNTY	DEM	PERCENT	REP	PERCENT	OTHER	PERCENT	TOTAL
Delaware	178,087	45.5%	164,578	42.1%	25,485	6.5%	391,224
Elk	8,925	46.5%	8,197	42.7%	1,026	5.3%	19,203
Erie	97,474	51.2%	67,674	35.5%	14,514	7.6%	190,394
Fayette	44,497	57.8%	25,819	33.5%	3,998	5.2%	76,971
Forest	1,269	38.2%	1,746	52.5%	155	4.7%	3,323
Franklin	23,957	26.6%	53,507	59.3%	9,215	10.2%	90,178
Fulton	2,430	27.0%	5,664	62.8%	521	5.8%	9,013
Greene	12,385	54.8%	8,138	36.0%	1,226	5.4%	22,606
Huntingdon	9,171	30.8%	17,482	58.8%	2,220	7.5%	29,745
Indiana	20,456	39.5%	24,200	46.8%	4,520	8.7%	51,731
Jefferson	9,467	31.7%	16,998	56.9%	1,727	5.8%	29,858
Juniata	3,961	28.6%	8,463	61.1%	998	7.2%	13,857
Lackawanna	86,883	61.6%	40,959	29.0%	9,612	6.8%	141,103
Lancaster	101,222	31.7%	168,315	52.7%	26,906	8.4%	319,324
Lawrence	25,937	47.8%	22,586	41.6%	3,188	5.9%	54,304
Lebanon	25,763	30.9%	45,984	55.1%	7,374	8.8%	83,416
Lehigh	109,437	48.6%	78,168	34.7%	28,767	12.8%	225,172
Luzerne	107,682	52.4%	74,285	36.2%	16,246	7.9%	205,338
Lycoming	21,236	31.6%	37,320	55.5%	5,065	7.5%	67,222
McKean	7,290	29.3%	14,158	56.9%	1,857	7.5%	24,862
Mercer	30,894	43.8%	30,761	43.6%	6,533	9.3%	70,530
Mifflin	7,557	29.2%	15,573	60.1%	1,945	7.5%	25,912
Monroe	51,935	47.4%	36,403	33.3%	12,514	11.4%	109,470
Montgomery	271,861	47.1%	215,343	37.3%	45,463	7.9%	577,005
Montour	4,747	36.2%	6,296	48.0%	1,438	11.0%	13,112
Northampton	98,750	46.7%	73,616	34.8%	23,989	11.3%	211,440
Northumber-land	19,624	37.6%	26,126	50.0%	3,414	6.5%	52,241
Perry	7,202	24.9%	18,216	62.9%	2,503	8.6%	28,949
Philadelphia	800,853	77.5%	117,952	11.4%	78,041	7.5%	1,033,979
Pike	13,997	34.7%	17,900	44.4%	4,754	11.8%	40,280
Potter	2,708	25.3%	6,933	64.7%	734	6.9%	10,709

(*Continued*)

Table 2.2 (*Continued*)

COUNTY	DEM	PERCENT	REP	PERCENT	OTHER	PERCENT	TOTAL
Schuylkill	32,303	38.0%	42,948	50.5%	4,951	5.8%	84,991
Snyder	5,564	25.0%	13,860	62.3%	1,983	8.9%	22,249
Somerset	17,468	35.2%	27,373	55.2%	2,862	5.8%	49,603
Sullivan	1,515	34.7%	2,392	54.8%	244	5.6%	4,362
Susquehanna	7,682	30.0%	14,685	57.4%	1,715	6.7%	25,567
Tioga	7,134	26.8%	15,961	59.9%	2,515	9.4%	26,638
Union	7,113	30.2%	12,521	53.1%	2,534	10.7%	23,579
Venango	10,475	33.4%	17,022	54.4%	2,044	6.5%	31,316
Warren	10,416	34.6%	15,126	50.3%	2,017	6.7%	30,094
Washington	67,798	48.8%	55,479	39.9%	11,351	8.2%	138,913
Wayne	9,622	29.7%	17,635	54.4%	3,747	11.6%	32,399
Westmoreland	112,689	45.9%	103,946	42.4%	15,249	6.2%	245,311
Wyoming	5,332	31.6%	9,614	56.9%	960	5.7%	16,891
York	102,561	34.6%	147,902	49.9%	35,731	12.0%	296,619
Totals	4,217,456	48.3%	3,301,182	37.8%	1,204,339	13.8%	8,722,977

Source: Pennsylvania Department of State.

The advantage that the Democrats have is based largely on their ability to accumulate big numbers in some of the urban areas of the state, especially within the cities of Philadelphia and Pittsburgh (Allegheny County). Philadelphia, where the Democrats have almost seven hundred thousand more registered voters, presents a formidable hurdle for the GOP, particularly in high-turnout presidential elections, when those voters are more likely to cast ballots. However, their support is also not limited to those two cities alone. Of the ten largest cities in the state, only one, Lancaster, which ranks eighth, is located within a county in which the Democrats do not hold an edge. As for counties themselves, of the fifteen most populated in the state, all but three—Lancaster, Chester, and York (sixth, seventh, and eighth, respectively)—have a Democratic edge. Conversely, of the fifteen least-populated counties, the Republicans have the advantage in all but Greene and Elk (fifth-eighth and fifty-ninth, respectively overall).

While these numbers place the Republicans at a certain disadvantage, it is not as insurmountable a climb as it may appear, for several reasons. First, evidence suggests that Democrats are more likely to split their tickets, crossing over and voting for Republican candidates, than for the reverse to occur.

Second, in low-turnout, midterm, and odd-year elections, Republicans are generally more likely to actually go to the polls than are Democrats. This helps explain why the GOP has been able to win stunning victories, both nationally and in Pennsylvania, in both the 2010 and

Table 2.3 Pennsylvania Voter Registration Totals Since 1950

YEAR	DEMOCRAT	PERCENT	REPUBLICAN	PERCENT	OTHER	PERCENT	TOTALS
1950	1,930,916	40.6%	2,772,778	58.2%	57,966	1.2%	4,761,660
1960	2,805,202	49.3%	2,802,237	49.3%	80,398	1.4%	5,687,837
1970	2,627,130	55.3%	2,008,411	42.3%	112,010	2.4%	4,747,551
1980	3,072,700	53.4%	2,374,677	41.3%	307,284	5.3%	5,754,661
1990	2,907,156	51.4%	2,476,222	43.8%	275,811	4.9%	5,659,189
2000	3,736,304	48.0%	3,250,764	41.8%	794,929	10.2%	7,781,997
2010	4,311,203	50.8%	3,132,039	36.9%	1,035,267	12.2%	8,478,509
2016	4,217,456	48.3%	3,301,182	37.8%	1,204,339	13.8%	8,722,977

Sources: *The Pennsylvania Manual* for years 1950–2010.

The Pennsylvania Department of State for 2016.

2014 midterm elections (with one outlier being the later gubernatorial election in the state). Additionally, in many instances (though not all), the Republican Party is better organized and their candidates better financed.

Looking back over several decades, Table 2.3 illustrates how significantly the state has changed since the partisan realignment of the 1950s. In the 1950s, the Republicans owned a sizeable advantage of the state's registered voters, with over 58 percent—an almost twenty-point gap separating them from the Democrats. By the end of that decade, their lead had been swept away, and the two parties were remarkably close, with the Democrats holding a three-thousand-registrant advantage out of over 5.6 million registered overall. The decade of the 1960s was a particularly good one for the Democrats, as they went from essentially being tied with the GOP to amassing a 13 percent advantage. The GOP made modest gains in the next three decades: they were eventually able to cut their deficit in half and were just a little more than six percentage points behind by the end of the twentieth century. However, a combination of forces, such as the unpopularity of President George W. Bush towards the end of his second term and the spirited 2008 presidential primary battle between Barack Obama and Hillary Clinton (the first time the state had been relevant in the nomination of either party in decades), spiked Democratic numbers to their highest share yet: close to fourteen percentage points. Since that time, the GOP has been able to marginally narrow the gap, yet they still trail their adversaries by 10.5 percentage points.

Perhaps the most intriguing change in recent decades has been the growth of registrants who are not members of either major party. In 1950, their numbers were miniscule, at just over 1 percent. A slight increase in subsequent decades has given way to a more significant one in recent years. Today, over 13 percent of Pennsylvania voters are not registered with either the Democratic Party or Republican Party. This is not an insignificant figure, since, as residents of a "closed party" primary state, they are unable to cast ballots in the spring primary elections, when the major party nominees are chosen. Clearly an increasing number of the state's voters are willing to concede this task as a way to demonstrate their independence or antipathy towards the two major parties.

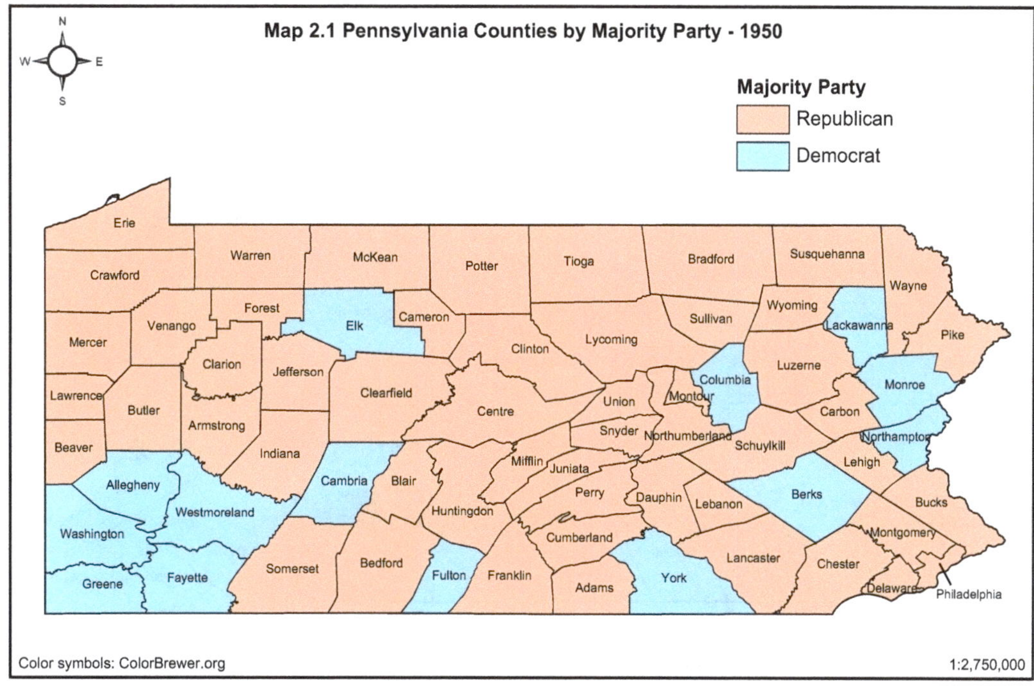

Map 2.1 Pennsylvania Counties by Majority Party, 1950

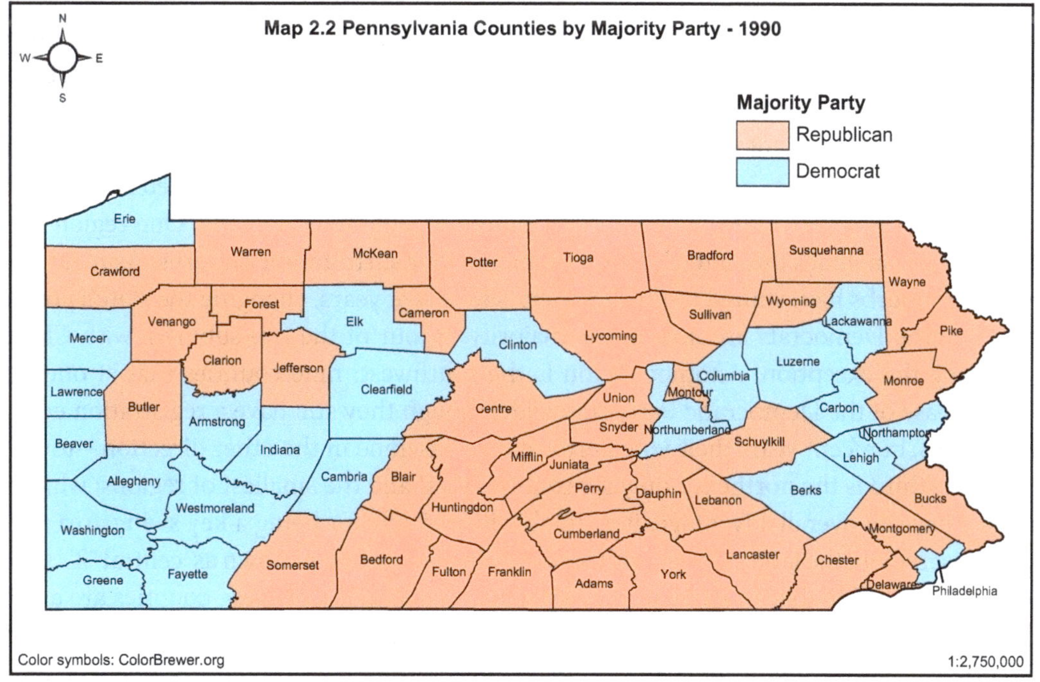

Map 2.2 Pennsylvania Counties by Majority Party, 1990

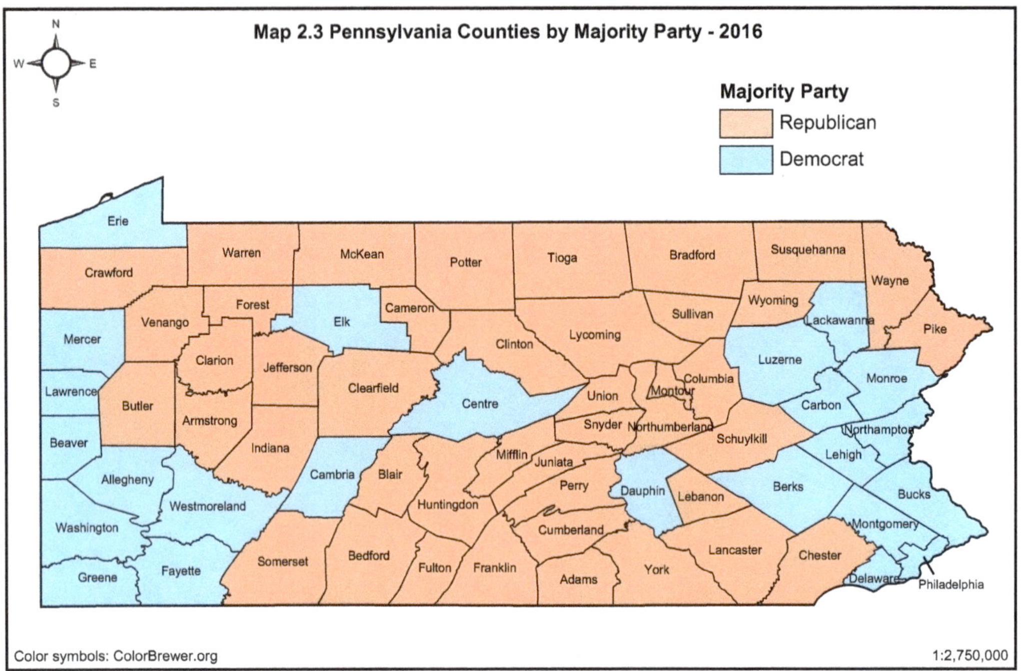

Map 2.3 Pennsylvania Counties by Majority Party, 2016

The maps included above illustrate the partisan breakdown in each of the state's sixty-seven counties at the time these important changes developed as well as a map detailing the current allocation.

One interesting and useful approach in analyzing voting patterns in Pennsylvania or any state is to view it through the lens of the state's geographic regions. In the book entitled *Pennsylvania Elections*, this author carved the state into four different geographic regions. One region is the southeast, which includes the state's largest city and its four surrounding suburbs. As mentioned above, these suburbs have shifted to the Democrats in recent years, changing the state's political equilibrium. The Democrats are now in the majority in four of the five suburbs, with Chester County being the exception. Another region is the southwest: nine counties that at one time formed the base of the Democratic Party statewide; though they still have a registration edge in seven counties, in recent years their vote performance has gone in the other direction—towards the GOP. The third is the northeast: only six counties total and the smallest of regions; while the Democrats have an overall advantage, it is notable historically for being a key swing area in the state. The last region, the largest by far with forty-seven counties and known as central "T," serves as the base for the Republican Party in Pennsylvania. While many of these counties are among the least populated in the state, when adding them all together, the total number of votes that the GOP is often able to garner overall can be considerable. Throughout these forty-seven counties, the Republicans hold the registration lead in all but seven.

Table 2.4 below lists each of the four major regions in the state and the details of how many counties in each the Democrats have a plurality in relative to the overall number in that particular region. The two years selected as a comparison, 1950 and 1990, were chosen because those were the two election cycles prior to the upcoming realignments. Again, the Democratic Party weakness is readily apparent when assessing the 1950 figures, as are the gains made by the party since that time. Today the Democrats have a plurality in twenty-four of the state's counties overall—a slight change over time, though there are some important shifts within the state. Again, the biggest change is found in the populous Philadelphia suburbs, where the Democrats have surged recently. While they have lost some ground in some areas, those tend to be much less populous, which accounts for their overall gains.

Table 2.4 Democratic Party Plurality of Registrants by Region

YEAR	SOUTHEAST	SOUTHWEST	NORTHEAST	CENTRAL "T"	TOTAL
1950	0/5	5/9	4/6	6/40	15/67
1990	1/5	8/9	5/6	10/40	22/67
2016	4/5	7/9	6/6	7/40	24/67

Sources: *The Pennsylvania Manual* for years 1950 and 1992.

The Pennsylvania Department of State for 2016.

As Map 2.4 demonstrates, there are some geographic liberties taken with this model. The "T" itself stretches hundreds of miles across the northern tier of the state, from Wayne County to

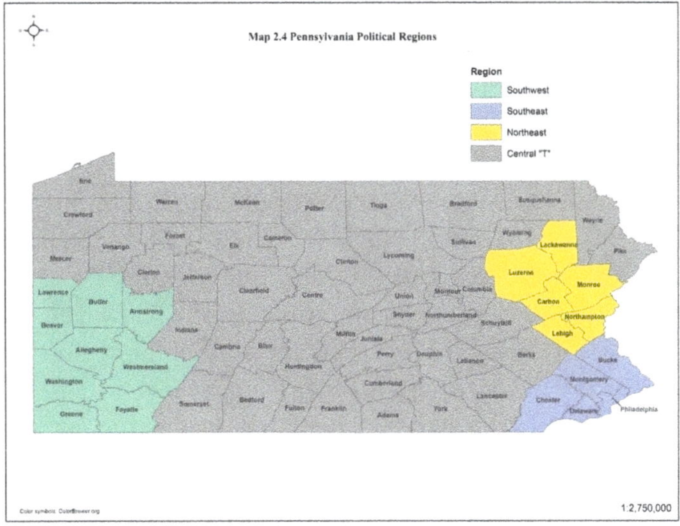

Map 2.4 Pennsylvania Political Regions

Erie County. At the southern border, it begins in Lancaster County (home to more Republicans than any other in the "T") and continues across the Maryland border until it reaches Somerset County, and together it captures everything in between. While geographically it seems rather illogical, it makes better sense when cultural factors are included. That's because these counties make up what is often described as Pennsylvania's Bible Belt. Again, the Democrats have some pockets of support here, owing to factors such as being the seat of the state government (Dauphin County), being historically distressed economically (Cambria County), and containing the largest institution of higher learning in the state (Penn State University in Centre County). Another such county is Erie, which is isolated in the far northwestern corner of the state, is relatively populated, and doesn't possess the "T"'s cultural dynamics. A case could also be made that Berks County, which contains the city of Reading, is more politically and culturally in tune with the southeast, as it is situated adjacent to these counties and is also a part of the Philadelphia media market.

The same can be said for several counties in what is listed as the northeast. The Lehigh Valley contains Lehigh, Northampton, and Monroe Counties as well as parts of Berks, Carbon, and Schuylkill Counties. Many of these residents identify with the southeast region due to their close proximity (roughly an hour's drive from southern Lehigh County to Philadelphia) and the fact that it also is a part of Philadelphia's media market. Certainly, the vast majority of those who reside here are more likely to associate themselves with the southeast counties than those in the Scranton (Lackawanna)-Wilkes-Barre (Luzurne) area. In part, the author originally chose to group these counties together since they once shared a number of economic and cultural characteristics, such as being home to large-scale manufacturing and trade unions, while also containing a heavily Pennsylvania German tradition that tended toward the more conservative side of the cultural spectrum. Simply put, this was at one time the home to many so-called Reagan Democrats, but that has changed in recent years, partly due to an influx of commuters from New York and New Jersey who have made the Lehigh Valley both more culturally liberal and Democratic Party oriented. Again, while one could take issue with several of these listings, when viewed in this manner, it can provide some interesting insight into the state's political landscape.

As previously mentioned, the most significant development in the state's political system has occurred in the Philadelphia suburbs. In 1950 (Table 2.5), the Republicans could claim a remarkable 81 percent of registered voters in these four counties. By 1992, their numbers had slipped, though they still held over 63 percent of registrants. However, a Democratic surge in the late 2000s now provides them with a plurality overall in the region and in all but Chester County individually. In the most populous county in the region (and the third most in the state), Montgomery, the Democrats have widened their lead to ten percentage points.

As for raw numbers, the Democrats have increased by 506,139 since 1992, as compared to 38,967 for the Republicans—a net increase for the Democrats of 467,172 in the region.

Table 2.5 Party Registration in the Southeast Suburbs Since 1950

1950							
COUNTY	DEMOCRATS	PERCENTAGE	REPUBLICAN	PERCENTAGE	OTHER	PERCENTAGE	TOTALS
Bucks	16,796	26.9%	43,012	69.0%	2,520	4.0%	62,328
Chester	13,042	21.3%	47,420	77.3%	877	1.4%	61,339
Delaware	23,998	11.5%	181,614	86.9%	3,456	1.7%	209,068
Montgomery	31,004	18.7%	131,603	79.4%	3,201	1.9%	165,808
SE Totals	84,840	17.0%	403,649	81.0%	10,054	2.0%	498,543
1992							
COUNTY	DEMOCRATS	PERCENTAGE	REPUBLICAN	PERCENTAGE	OTHER	PERCENTAGE	TOTALS
Bucks	105,854	39.7%	140,365	52.6%	20,716	7.8%	266,935
Chester	45,534	26.0%	112,897	64.5%	16,545	9.5%	174,976
Delaware	72,753	24.3%	209,792	70.0%	17,067	5.7%	299,612
Montgomery	98,105	28.8%	216,509	63.6%	25,588	7.5%	340,202
SE Totals	322,246	29.8%	679,563	62.8%	79,916	7.4%	1,081,725
2016							
COUNTY	DEMOCRATS	PERCENTAGE	REPUBLICAN	PERCENTAGE	OTHER	PERCENTAGE	TOTALS
Bucks	190,862	46.5%	179,940	43.9%	39,322	9.6%	410,124
Chester	129,234	42.0%	149,589	48.6%	28,739	9.3%	307,562
Delaware	178,249	48.0%	168,124	45.3%	24,874	6.7%	371,247
Montgomery	257,956	51.0%	208,044	41.2%	39,463	7.8%	505,463
SE Totals	828,385	48.9%	718,530	42.5%	145,461	8.6%	1,692,376

Sources: *The Pennsylvania Manual* for years 1950 and 1992.
The Pennsylvania Department of State for 2016.

Those categorized as "Other" party in the region even outgained the GOP with 65,545 more registrants.

However, these Democratic gains in the southeast have not occurred in isolation, and the cultural issues that have contributed to this shift have also negatively impacted their performance in the more socially conservative southwest. Since 1992, the Democratic Party registration has slipped eleven percentage points, and while non-major-party registrants have

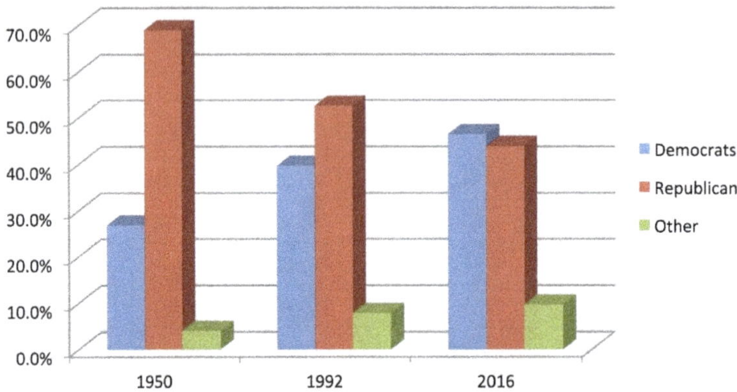

Figure 2.1 Bucks County Registration Since 1950

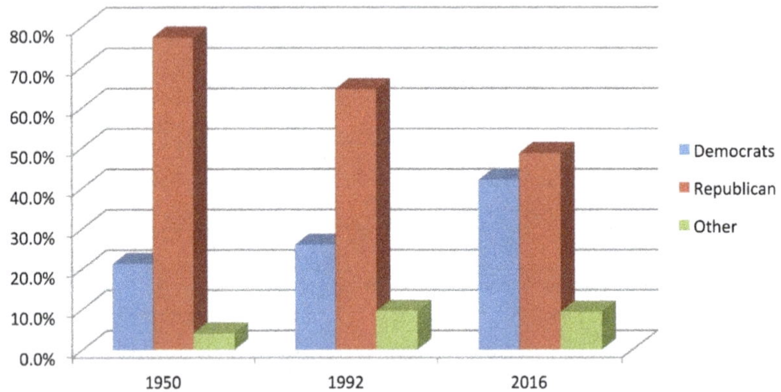

Figure 2.2 Chester County Registration Since 1950

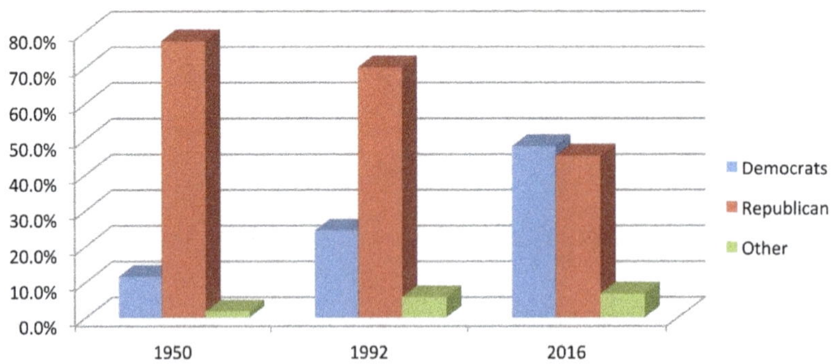

Figure 2.3 Delaware County Registration Since 1950

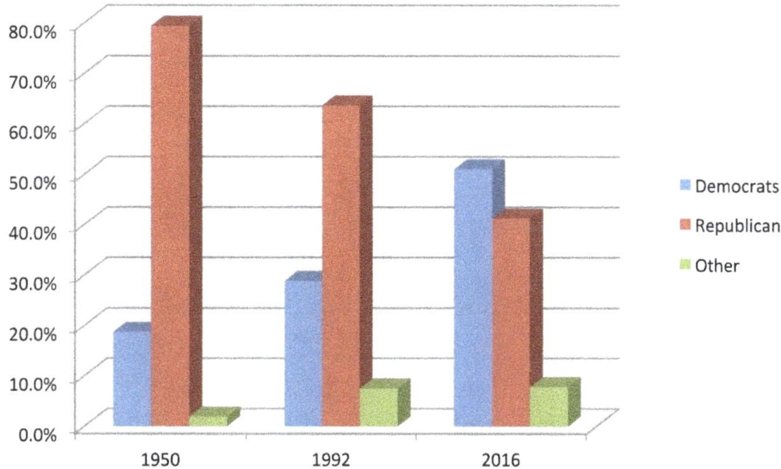

Figure 2.4 Montgomery County Registration Since 1950

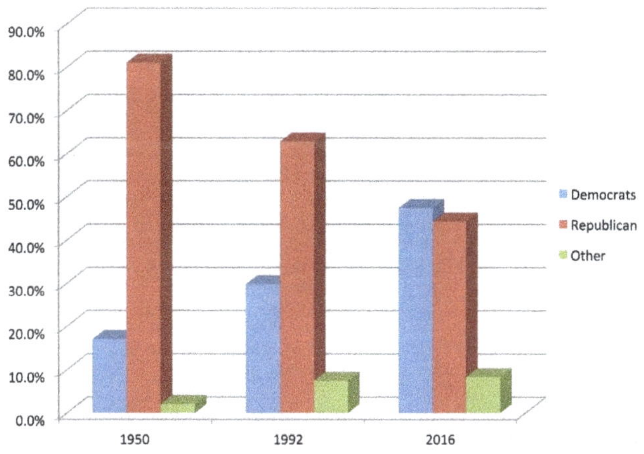

Figure 2.5 Southeast Registration Since 1950

slightly increased, most of the movement has been towards the Republicans (Table 2.6). As for raw numbers in this region, it is a mirror image of what has occurred in the southeast. Here, the Democrats have added only 44,385 voters since 1992, lag behind the number of "Other" party registrants (which increased by 69,517), and badly trail the Republicans, who've increased by 229,176. This marks a net increase for the Republicans in the region of 184,791 registrants over the Democrats since 1992. Again, these totals don't match the overall numbers by which the Democrats have increased in the southeast, but it does illustrate clearly the different directions in which these two areas now seem to be going politically.

Table 2.6 Party Registration in the Southwest Since 1950

1950							
COUNTY	DEMOCRATS	PERCENTAGE	REPUBLICAN	PERCENTAGE	OTHER	PERCENTAGE	TOTALS
Allegheny	451,910	59.0%	309,441	40.4%	3,960	0.5%	765,311
Armstrong	12,539	37.5%	20,789	62.1%	124	0.4%	33,452
Beaver	29,386	41.4%	40,914	57.6%	675	1.0%	70,975
Butler	13,566	33.8%	26,326	65.6%	244	0.6%	40,136
Fayette	51,285	62.7%	30,218	36.9%	305	0.4%	81,808
Greene	13,367	72.0%	5,180	27.9%	26	0.1%	18,573
Lawrence	14,741	32.1%	30,752	67.0%	386	0.8%	45,879
Washington	64,163	63.3%	36,852	36.4%	349	0.3%	101,364
Westmoreland	90,546	62.8%	53,095	36.8%	576	0.4%	144,217
Totals	741,503	57.0%	553,567	42.5%	6,645	0.5%	1,301,715
1992							
COUNTY	DEMOCRATS	PERCENTAGE	REPUBLICAN	PERCENTAGE	OTHER	PERCENTAGE	TOTALS
Allegheny	485,932	67.8%	196,499	27.4%	34,470	4.8%	716,901
Armstrong	16,753	52.1%	14,460	45.0%	927	2.9%	32,140
Beaver	62,440	68.5%	25,023	27.5%	3,687	4.0%	91,150
Butler	30,139	45.7%	32,044	48.6%	3,758	5.7%	65,941
Fayette	50,213	78.0%	12,792	19.9%	1,339	2.1%	64,344
Greene	13,873	79.0%	3,469	19.8%	222	1.3%	17,564
Lawrence	26,452	58.3%	17,295	38.1%	1,626	3.6%	45,373
Washington	67,744	69.5%	25,827	26.5%	3,894	4.0%	97,465
Westmoreland	115,390	67.4%	48,665	28.4%	7,211	4.2%	171,266
Totals	868,936	66.7%	376,074	28.9%	57,134	4.4%	1,302,144
2016							
COUNTY	DEMOCRATS	PERCENTAGE	REPUBLICAN	PERCENTAGE	OTHER	PERCENTAGE	TOTALS
Allegheny	520,006	62.5%	246,022	29.6%	65,416	7.9%	831,444
Armstrong	15,832	41.1%	20,434	53.0%	2,278	5.9%	38,544
Beaver	58,855	57.6%	38,020	37.2%	5,239	5.1%	102,114
Butler	41,167	35.6%	65,265	56.4%	9,351	8.1%	115,783

(*Continued*)

Table 2.6 (*Continued*)

COUNTY	DEMOCRATS	PERCENTAGE	REPUBLICAN	PERCENTAGE	OTHER	PERCENTAGE	TOTALS
Fayette	48,796	62.8%	25,120	32.3%	3,805	4.9%	77,721
Greene	12,615	60.2%	7,235	34.5%	1,094	5.2%	20,944
Lawrence	27,408	52.6%	21,798	41.8%	2,893	5.6%	52,099
Washington	66,805	52.4%	50,570	39.6%	10,169	8.0%	127,544
Westmoreland	117,450	50.9%	99,027	42.9%	14,394	6.2%	230,871
Totals	913,321	55.5%	605,250	36.8%	126,651	7.7%	1,645,222

Sources: *The Pennsylvania Manual* for years 1950 and 1992.

The Pennsylvania Department of State for 2016.

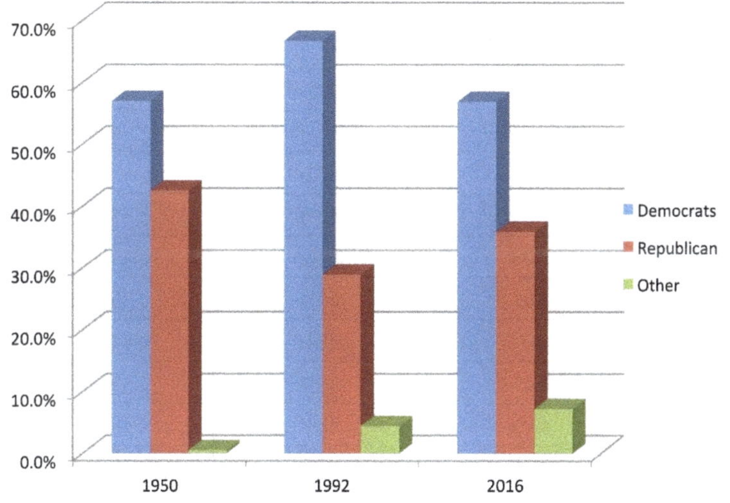

Figure 2.6 Southwest Registration Since 1950

PRESIDENTIAL ELECTIONS IN PENNSYLVANIA

Once Pennsylvania became two-party competitive in the 1950s, it would for decades epitomize what political observers characterize as a battleground state. It contained all of the ingredients: it was representative of the national vote, highly competitive, and possessing a large block of electoral votes, all of which attracted candidates to the state in their attempts to court their voters.

On the first matter (representative of the national vote), the state has been remarkably consistent ever since the Democrats began to challenge Republicans in the state. As Table 2.7 illustrates, in the seventeen presidential elections that have occurred since 1952, the Democrats have performed better in thirteen of them, while in three elections the percentage that the victorious party received matched the national number. The only exception to this is the most recent election, in which Republican Donald Trump's share of the vote in Pennsylvania eclipsed that of his national total. Interestingly, each of these four exceptions has occurred every twenty years: 1956, 1976, 1996, and 2016. However, in those other thirteen contests in which the Democrats have had the advantage, only a few have ranged outside of three percentage points: 1964 (four points), 1968 (five points), and 1984 (six points). Since that 1984 contest, in which President Reagan won by eighteen points nationally (compared with a relatively more modest seven-point win in the Keystone State), the spread has been no greater than three percentage points for the winner. Overall, in these sixteen elections, the Democrats' share in the state has averaged slightly over two percentage points higher than the national total. Overall, the Democrats have carried the state in ten of the seventeen presidential elections held since Pennsylvania became a two-party state in the early 1950s.

Table 2.7 Comparison of Presidential Elections in Pennsylvania to National Results

	NATIONAL		PENNSYLVANIA		
YEAR	DEMOCRAT	REPUBLICAN	DEMOCRAT	REPUBLICAN	MARGIN
1952	44%	55%	47%	53%	D+2
1956	42%	57%	43%	57%	EVEN
1960	50%	50%	51%	49%	D+1
1964	61%	39%	65%	35%	D+4
1968*	43%	43%	48%	44%	D+5
1972	38%	61%	39%	59%	D+2
1976	50%	48%	50%	48%	EVEN
1980	41%	51%	43%	50%	D+1
1984	41%	59%	46%	53%	D+6
1988	46%	53%	48%	51%	D+2
1992	43%	37%	45%	36%	D+2
1996	49%	41%	49%	40%	EVEN
2000*	48%	48%	51%	46%	D+3
2004	48%	51%	51%	48%	D+3
2008	53%	46%	55%	44%	D+2
2012	51%	47%	52%	47%	D+1
2016	48%	46%	48%	49%	R+3

*Indicates year when Pennsylvania's winner differed from national winner.

Source: USElectionsatlas.org.

While still considered a battleground state, prior to the 2016 election it appeared that Pennsylvania's status as such was becoming increasingly tenuous. For instance, from 1952–1996, the state cast its lot with the eventual winner in all but one election—in 1968, when the state went narrowly for Vice President Hubert H. Humphrey over Richard Nixon. In 2000, along with the states of Florida and Michigan, Pennsylvania was still viewed by most as one of the three big prizes right up until Election Day, with both candidates, Vice President Al Gore and Texas governor George W. Bush, spending considerable amounts of time and money in the state. In somewhat of a surprise, however, the Democrat carried the state by 205,000 votes (a four-point victory) despite losing the overall election. However, considering the fact that Al Gore actually won the popular vote that year, it does take some of the sting out of the fact that the state ran counter to the nation.

Four years later, however, though it was close, then-president Bush scored a clearer victory nationally over Massachusetts senator John Kerry. Despite a major effort by Bush, who invested plenty in Pennsylvania (making forty-two trips to the state during his first term), the Democrats again carried the state, further dealing the state a blow to its battleground status. By 2012, the GOP had seemingly written off the state from the beginning, ignoring it almost until the very end. Outside of a few fundraising visits, their candidate, former Massachusetts governor Mitt Romney, didn't stage a rally in the state until November 4, on the Sunday before the election, in Bucks County. Despite this effort, which wildly raised hopes among Romney's supporters, incumbent President Barack Obama easily won the state by roughly three hundred thousand votes. The Democrats' victory in 2012 marked the sixth straight time the Democrats have carried the state in presidential elections, raising serious questions that the state is no longer a true battleground. While not a true blue state, it does appear to be a rather deep purple at this particular time in its history. Overall, the Democrats have carried the state in ten of the sixteen presidential elections held since the last major party realignment of the 1950s and, of course, all six since the more minor one, which occurred in the early 1990s.

The main reason accounting for this Democratic winning streak is the realigning shift that has occurred in the four Philadelphia suburbs since the 1992 presidential election. Prior to that time, only Lyndon Johnson in his 1964 landslide win was able to carry this combined suburban vote. A 206,000-vote plurality in these suburbs was critical to George H.W. Bush's victory over Michael Dukakis in their 1988 contest, one in which the Republican carried the state by just slightly more than 105,000 votes. Four years later, however, it was the Democratic candidate, Bill Clinton, who carried three of the four counties, losing only Chester, en route to a three-thousand-vote plurality overall. The growing impact that this change has brought upon the state's politics is illustrated in Table 2.8.

Since that time, the Democrats have continued to improve their performance in the Philadelphia suburbs. In fact, despite losing statewide in 2016, Democratic nominee Hillary Clinton amassed a plurality of over 663,000 votes in the five-county region. Ordinarily, that would have been more than enough to comfortably carry Pennsylvania; however, 2016 was certainly no ordinary year. Few could have predicted what she would run up against throughout the rest of the commonwealth.

Table 2.8 Presidential Election Results in Southeastern Pennsylvania

YEAR	SE SUBURBS	SE SUBURBS PLUS PHILADELPHIA	STATEWIDE
1988	R+ 206,000	D+ 2,000	R+ 105,000
1992	D+ 3,000	D+ 304,000	D+ 447,000
1996	D+ 42,000	D+ 370,000	D+ 415,000
2000	D+ 54,000	D+ 403,000	D+ 205,000
2004	D+ 87,000	D+ 500,000	D+ 144,000
2008	D+ 204,000	D+ 683,000	D+ 620,000
2012	D+ 123,000	D+ 616,000	D+ 310,000
2016	D+ 188,353	D+ 663,630	R+ 44,292

Sources: *The Pennsylvania Manual* for years 1988–2012.
The Pennsylvania Department of State for 2016.

While Democrats have increased their advantages in the southeast, they are clearly hemorrhaging support across much of the rest of Pennsylvania. This was never clearer than it was in the 2016 presidential election, beginning with the southwestern part of the state. This area was once a Democratic stronghold, but Donald Trump was able to carry the nine counties in this region by almost seventy-five thousand votes. Table 2.9 presents a startling contrast, as Michael Dukakis actually carried the southwest rather handily by over two hundred thousand

Table 2.9 Presidential Election Results in Southwestern Pennsylvania

YEAR	SOUTHWEST	STATEWIDE
1988	D+ 201,000	R+ 105,000
1992	D+ 245,000	D+ 447,000
1996	D+ 121,000	D+ 415,000
2000	D+ 88,000	D+ 205,000
2004	D+ 49,000	D+ 144,000
2008	D+ 29,000	D+ 620,000
2012	R+ 20,000	D+ 310,000
2016	R+ 75,996	R+ 44,292

Sources: *The Pennsylvania Manual* for years 1988–2012.
The Pennsylvania Department of State for 2016.

votes in his overall losing effort back in 1988. Clinton expanded that to a 245,000-vote margin four years later; however, it was after that the Democratic margins began to decline and eventually disappear at the presidential level. Barack Obama could only muster a 29,000-vote edge while easily carrying the state by 620,000 votes in 2008, and he even lost the region as a whole in his reelection effort—the first time that the Democrats had lost the region since the Nixon/McGovern landslide in 1972. Even Walter Mondale was able to carry the southwest by over 150,000 votes in 1984 against Ronald Reagan.

This realignment has also more modestly impacted the northeast industrial region. As Table 2.10 illustrates, after George H.W. Bush outpolled Dukakis in these six counties back in 1988, the area had consistently voted Democratic at the presidential level, largely reflecting their overall registration advantage. However, Donald Trump was also able to carry this region by almost thirty thousand votes. Between the southwest and northeast, both traditionally Democratic, the GOP was able to register a plurality of slightly over one hundred thousand votes, easily enough to make up the margin of victory. It should be noted that the overall numbers produced in this region continue to be more reflective of the state than any other region.

Table 2.10 Presidential Election Results in Northeastern Pennsylvania

YEAR	NORTHEAST	STATEWIDE
1988	R+ 23,000	R+ 105,000
1992	D+ 31,000	D+ 447,000
1996	D+ 49,000	D+ 415,000
2000	D+ 39,000	D+ 205,000
2004	D+ 25,000	D+ 144,000
2008	D+ 91,000	D+ 620,000
2012	D+ 57,000	D+ 310,000
2016	R+ 29,743	R+ 44,292

Sources: *The Pennsylvania Manual* for years 1988–2012.
The Pennsylvania Department of State for 2016.

In fact, Northampton County, which contains the cities of Bethlehem and Easton, is the clearest bellwether that Pennsylvania has, as far as a county is concerned, in being able to predict what will happen across the rest of the state. Below, Table 2.11 traces the Democratic share of the presidential vote in this county as compared to the overall state average since 1980. Remarkably, only in the 1992 three-way contest between Clinton, Bush, and Perot did this county's vote differ from the state figure by more than one percentage point, and even then, it was only two points off. In the ten presidential elections conducted

Table 2.11 Presidential Election Results in Northampton County

YEAR	NORTHAMPTON COUNTY	STATEWIDE
1980	42%	43%
1984	46%	46%
1988	47%	48%
1992	43%	45%
1996	48%	49%
2000	51%	51%
2004	50%	51%
2008	55%	55%
2012	52%	52%
2016	50%	49%

Sources: *The Pennsylvania Manual* for years 1988–2012.

The Pennsylvania Department of State for 2016.

since 1980, Northampton County has produced the exact same percentage of the vote for the overall winner in four of them. No question; if you want to know how Pennsylvania's voters are going to perform overall, you need not look any further than this county situated along the New Jersey border.

The last region of the state, the central "T," has remained untouched by any changes that have occurred since the early 1990s in the state's electorate and, in fact, have remained basically the same for well over a century—that is, solidly Republican. As Table 2.12 shows, the GOP depends upon these forty-seven counties to provide a big chunk of votes, and rarely do they fail to deliver. Trump's margin of over 602,000 votes is a remarkable achievement, even in this conservative region. Few predicted that it would be so overwhelming as to help send Donald Trump to the White House, but indeed it did.

Previously, in only the two elections in the 1990s, with the presence of H. Ross Perot on the ballot as a third-party candidate siphoning off votes, did the GOP's margins noticeably decline. Otherwise, in a normal election, the best that a Democratic candidate for president could probably hope for in the central "T" is the 182,000-vote loss that Barack Obama experienced in his initial run against Senator John McCain in 2008. Maps 2.5, 2.6, and 2.7 illustrate how the voting patterns of Pennsylvanians have shifted between 1992 and 2016 presidential elections, with Democratic success in the southeast suburbs counterbalanced (though not yet by enough) by Republican gains in the southwest.

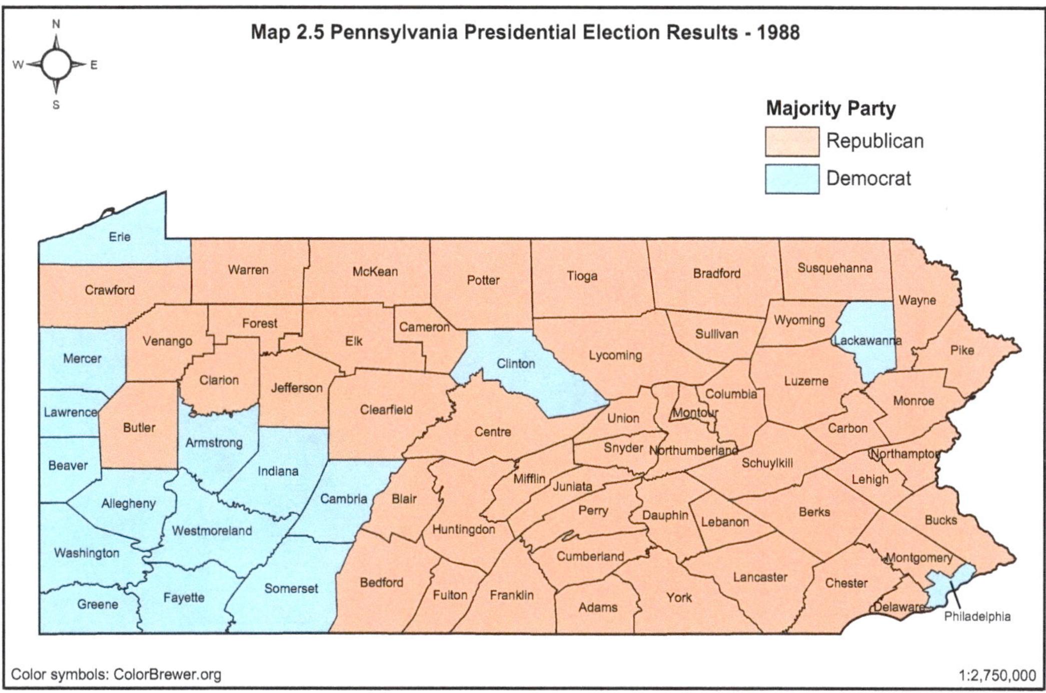

Map 2.5 Pennsylvania Presidential Election Results, 1988

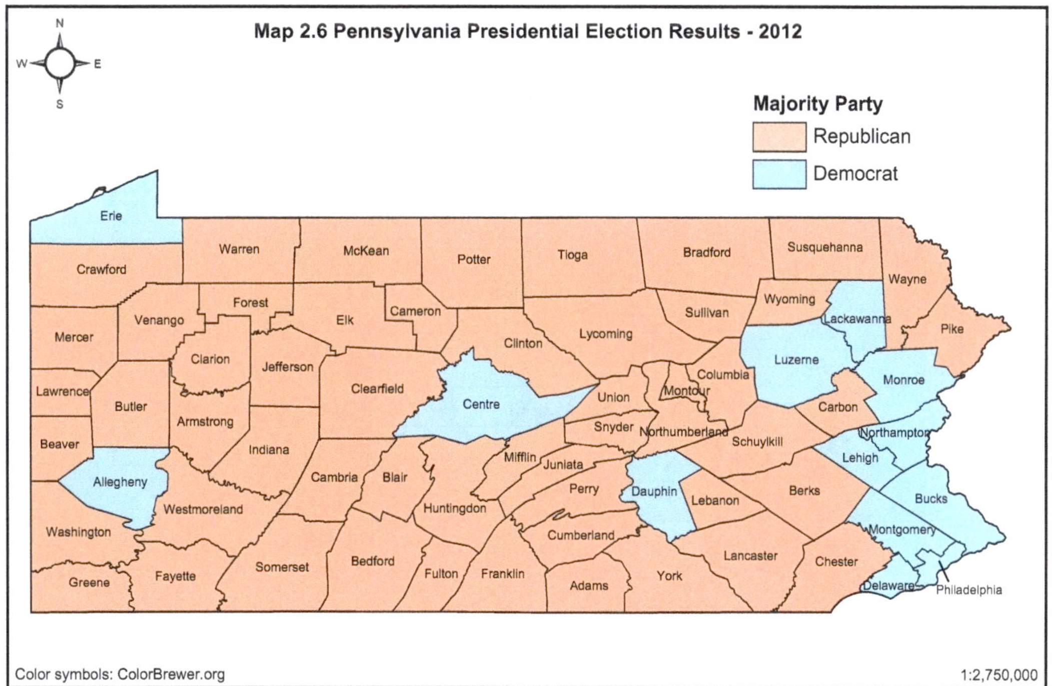

Map 2.6 Pennsylvania Presidential Election Results, 2012

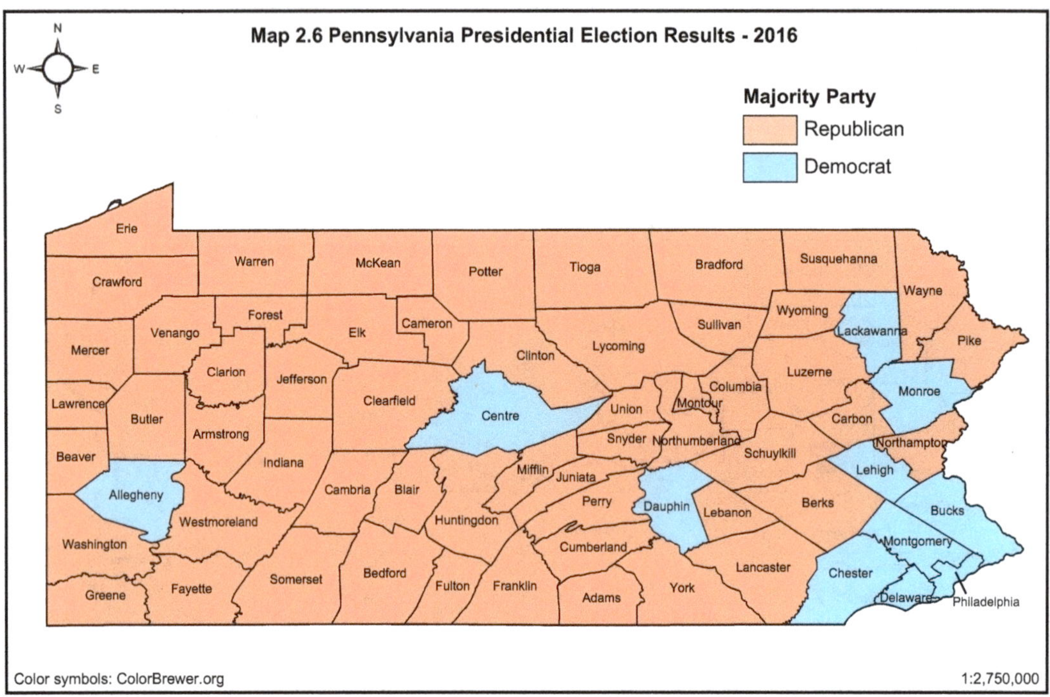

Map 2.7 Pennsylvania Presidential Election Results, 2016

Table 2.12 Presidential Elections Results in Pennsylvania's Central "T"

YEAR	CENTRAL "T"	STATEWIDE
1988	R+ 307,000	R+ 105,000
1992	R+ 133,000	D+ 447,000
1996	R+ 125,000	D+ 415,000
2000	R+ 325,000	D+ 205,000
2004	R+ 428,000	D+ 144,000
2008	R+ 182,000	D+ 620,000
2012	R+ 342,000	D+ 310,000
2016	R+ 602,183	R+ 44,292

Sources: *The Pennsylvania Manual* for years 1988–2012.

The Pennsylvania Department of State for 2016.

Finally, although Pennsylvania has seemingly regained its reputation as a battleground state, it should be mentioned that it has witnessed a decline in its overall clout. In 1952, Pennsylvania had thirty-two electoral votes—more than any state save for New York and the same number as California. Currently it possesses just twenty, a significant decline. It has also been eclipsed by Florida and Texas in addition to the two states listed above, and it has the same number as Illinois. On a positive note, the state's electoral decline may have been slowed, if not totally arrested. Following the 2010 census, Pennsylvania lost only one electoral vote (the first time that it didn't lose at least two in seventy years) in the reapportionment that followed the 1940 census.

GUBERNATORIAL ELECTIONS IN PENNSYLVANIA

One of the most intriguing aspects of elections in Pennsylvania over the last half century has been the eight-year switch in control of the state's chief executive, beginning at the time when the state became competitive politically. The election of Democrat George Leader in the fall of 1954 perhaps contributed more than anything, save the dramatic partisan change in Philadelphia, to creating a two-party system in the state. Leader, a state senator from York County, was the first Democrat to be elected governor in the state since George Earle in 1934; this came on the heels of the New Deal itself. Prior to that, only one other Democrat had been elected governor since the end of the Civil War: Robert Pattison, who served two nonconsecutive terms in the late 1800s.

Leader's victory came in spite of the overwhelming advantage that the Republicans had at that time, with more than nine hundred thousand registered voters across the state. In a state that had the type of multiplying effect that Pennsylvania did at that time (due to patronage), the Democrats would increase their share by roughly five points by the time he left office and would reach a slight majority by the end of the decade after he was succeeded by former Pittsburgh Mayor David Lawrence. This period of eight years in the political wilderness was the longest stretch for the GOP since their party was formed a century earlier, and they came roaring back with back-to-back victories for Congressman William Scranton in 1962 and his lieutenant governor, Ray Shafer, four years later.

After a change implemented at the Constitutional Convention of 1968, Pennsylvania's governors would thereafter be able to serve two terms rather than being limited to one. In the election of 1970, Democrats once again nominated Philadelphia-area businessman Milton Shapp (he had been their defeated candidate in 1966), and this time he won rather handily, as he did in his subsequent reelection. The 1978 open-seat campaign was a wild affair in a primary that featured seven Republicans and four Democrats. In both cases, geography was prominent, and two westerners emerged: Allegheny County District Attorney Richard Thornburgh for the Republicans and Pittsburgh Mayor Pete Flaherty for the Democrats. This campaign was also unique in the sense that the normal political coalitions were strained, as many labor groups supported the GOP candidate rather than the political maverick, Flaherty, whose policies as mayor had rankled many union supporters. Many prominent black clergy leaders in Philadelphia and even national leaders such as Reverend Jesse Jackson supported Republican Thornburgh as well. Despite the registration the Democrats had at this time of over nine hundred thousand registered voters, Flaherty's lead, which was measured at roughly thirty points following the primary, slipped away, and Thornburgh pulled off a surprising upset.

Thornburgh's reelection, however, was atypical and the only one in Pennsylvania prior to 2012, which was closely contested. His opponent was Congressman Allen Ertel from Lycoming County, located smack in the center of the "T." While this didn't provide Ertel much in the form of a traditional base, it did give him the opportunity to do better in central Pennsylvania, which he did, losing by only ten points in the region. However, the most significant obstacle for Thornburgh was the economy. Pennsylvania was in the midst of a recession, like the rest of the nation but even worse as the state's manufacturing sector experienced a sudden decline. Ultimately, Thornburgh prevailed by just 2 percent in his reelection bid and went on to serve as United States Attorney General after having been appointed by the Bush Administration in 1988.

The Republican candidate chosen to succeed him was Lieutenant Governor William Scranton III, son of the popular former governor. Scranton was viewed by many as a rising star, not just within the commonwealth but nationally as well. His opponent, Robert Casey, the former auditor-general, had been in Pennsylvania politics for decades, and he had been defeated in his three previous bids for the Democratic Party's nomination for governor. In one of the toughest and nastiest campaigns, even by Pennsylvania standards, Casey won by a narrow margin of eighty thousand votes. Similar to the 1978 contest, this was a race that defied convention as the more socially moderate Scranton racked up support from many traditional Democratic support groups while Casey made inroads among conservatives. Most observers attribute Casey's victory to what would become arguably the most famous campaign advertisement in the state's history. Dubbed the "guru ad," it aired on the weekend prior to the election, showing a picture of a younger Scranton, with long hair and a beard, meditating to the sounds of sitar music. There's little question that it played a part in driving down Scranton's support in central Pennsylvania, which was ultimately critical to his defeat.

Casey followed that with a landslide victory in 1990 over State Auditor-General Barbara Hafer, one in which he carried every county in the state except for Montgomery. The issue of legalized abortion rights dominated the debate, and it had the net benefit of helping the incumbent. In what was a reversal of the usual coalitions, Casey's pro-life stance was able to attract large numbers of Republicans to support his cause; however, Hafer's strong pro-choice position failed to similarly draw Democratic Party support. The Republicans came back behind Erie Congressman Tom Ridge in 1994. The Democratic candidate, Lieutenant Governor Mark Singel, had broken with the staunchly pro-life Casey on that issue two years earlier in his failed bid for the Democratic nomination for United States Senate, and the two never reconciled, which cost the Democrat support among some partisans. Perhaps more daunting, however, was that the political atmosphere in that particular year was toxic for Democrats; in what was President Clinton's first midterm election, they lost control of both houses of Congress for the first time since the 1954 election.

Ridge easily defeated Democratic state representative Ivan Itkin in 1998, and he resigned in his last year in office after being tapped by President George W. Bush to be the nation's first Secretary of Homeland Security following the terrorist attacks on September 11, 2001. Despite receiving general high marks in his limited time as the state's chief executive but perhaps not trying to defy the state's eight-year swing, Lieutenant Governor Mark Schweiker decided not to run for the job the following year. In retrospect, he perhaps would have been a more formidable candidate than State Senator Mike Fisher, who the GOP eventually selected. After a bruising primary battle in which he defeated State Treasurer Robert Casey Jr., Philadelphia Mayor Ed Rendell led Fisher from the start of the campaign and won rather easily. Rendell was perhaps even more popular in the southeast suburbs than he was in his home city, and his ability, in both the primary and general election, to roll up big margins in the southeast region proved insurmountable. He coasted to reelection over former Pittsburgh Steelers Hall of Fame wide receiver Lynn Swann. Swann's political inexperience showed and highlighted the fact that GOP leaders who rallied around his campaign in the spring—at the expense of former Lieutenant Governor Scranton, who was attempting a political comeback—were probably misguided.

Out of office for eight years and in the midst of an election cycle that was similar to what they faced in 1994, Democrats' chances of retaining control appeared slim in 2010. Their candidate was Allegheny County Executive Dan Onorato, who was little known in the eastern part of the state, and his inability to raise sufficient funds limited his ability to make an impression beyond his geographical base. The Republicans selected State Attorney General Tom Corbett, who was also from the Pittsburgh area but, unlike the Democrat, was well known throughout the state, particularly for prosecuting a number of politicos from both sides of the aisle for illegally engaging in electioneering while on public time.

Nevertheless, the eight-year pendulum swing was about to end. Despite a GOP-controlled legislature, the governor was unable to accomplish most of his more ambitious agenda items, such as privatization of the state's liquor system and pension reform. He publicly fought with legislative leaders of his own party and proved less than adept in front of the media, making several embarrassing and politically damaging gaffes, such as when, in defending a bill to mandate ultrasounds for women seeking abortions, he suggested that they just "close your eyes."[20] After a number of Democrats lined up to challenge him in 2014, York businessman Tom Wolf catapulted out of obscurity with a number of clever political ads highlighting his common touch in relation to his prized Jeep pickup. Corbett had difficulty landing any blows against Wolf, who had no political record to attack, and, despite it being another great environment for the GOP, Corbett became the first governor to fail to win reelection in the modern era, thus ending the eight-year switch. The public's perception of Wolf's battles with the still-GOP-controlled legislature will no doubt be central to whether the state reverts back to its former model or sets ahead toward a new one—that is, bouncing their chief executive after only one term.

So what accounts for this eight-year swing? Probably a combination of several factors. First, this is a highly competitive state, despite the advantage in party registration that the Democrats have enjoyed over the last several decades; some of this advantage is mitigated by partisans who are either more likely to cross party lines on Election Day or stay home altogether, especially in midterm elections. Second is the fact that gubernatorial elections in Pennsylvania take place (like thirty-six other states) during a midterm, and not a presidential, year, when the personalities and issues that so engulf those contests leak into a state's elections. Without question, when election for the state's chief executive is on the ballot every four years, it is the grand prize, with all the benefits and even the patronage that still exists, no matter what else is at stake, even contests for the United States Senate. Third, with some exception—perhaps Allen Ertel in 1982 (though even then, a better candidate might have defeated Governor Thornburgh)—the opposition party has had a difficult time recruiting top-tier challengers to take on the incumbent. Candidates such as Ivan Itkin or Lynn Swan had little chance from the very beginning to be successful, and their party and supporters were either duplicitous or delusional to believe otherwise. When a truly vulnerable incumbent finally appeared, the Democrats were fortunate enough to nominate a candidate who could exploit the situation, and Tom Wolf certainly did that in 2014. Table 2.13 below lists each of the governors who have served the state since 1950, along with their home county and party affiliation.

Table 2.13 Pennsylvania's Elected Governors Since 1950

YEAR	GOVERNOR	COUNTY	PARTY
1950	John Fine	Luzerne	Republican
1954	George Leader	York	Democrat
1958	David Lawrence	Allegheny	Democrat
1962	William Scranton	Lackawanna	Republican
1966	Ray Shafer	Crawford	Republican
1970	Milton Shapp	Philadelphia	Democrat
1974	Milton Shapp	Philadelphia	Democrat
1978	Richard Thornburgh	Allegheny	Republican
1982	Richard Thornburgh	Allegheny	Republican
1986	Robert Casey	Lackawanna	Democrat
1990	Robert Casey	Lackawanna	Democrat
1994	Tom Ridge	Erie	Republican
1998	Tom Ridge	Erie	Republican
2002	Ed Rendell	Philadelphia	Democrat
2006	Ed Rendell	Philadelphia	Democrat
2010	Tom Corbett	Allegheny	Republican
2014	Tom Wolf	York	Democrat

UNITED STATES SENATE ELECTIONS IN PENNSYLVANIA

The seesaw effect that took place at the gubernatorial level would have been a dream scenario for the Democrats, in retrospect, as it pertains to election to the United States Senate. Senate elections had been a veritable wasteland for the Democrats, particularly between the years 1968 and 2006. For almost forty years, the party could only muster a special election victory that allowed them to hold a senate seat for three years. That marked a degree of futility that

Image 2.1 Philadelphia Mayor and US Senator Joseph Clark

the Democratic Party didn't face anywhere else in the nation, not even in the staunchest Republican bastions, such as Idaho, Utah, or Wyoming. What qualifies this as one of the most dubious achievements in electoral politics is the fact that, through much of that time, the Democrats held not just a registration advantage but, at times, a sizeable one.

Beginning in 1950, the Democrats got off to a rough start with the defeat of two-term incumbent Francis Myers, a New Dealer first elected in 1938. Myers, the Democratic majority whip in the Senate, was also the first Roman Catholic ever elected to that institution from Pennsylvania. However, with President Truman's popularity in decline as the threat of Chinese advancement in Korea loomed, Democrats nationally paid the price in this midterm, and Myers was easily defeated by the progressive Republican governor, James Duff.

However, by the time Duff sought reelection in 1956, politics within the state had changed considerably, with the Democrats inching closer to being on a par with the Republicans with respect to party registration. The individual Duff faced was also one of the main reasons for the Democrats' rise: former Philadelphia mayor Joe Clark's victory five years earlier had upended the GOP machine in the state's largest city to the extent that it still has never recovered. Despite a big Republican wave across the state (led by President Eisenhower, who was winning reelection), enough voters who had been alienated by Duff over the years "cut" him from the ticket, allowing Clark to win in one of the closest contests ever imagined. The final results could not be determined until military ballots were counted after Election Day, but, in the end, Clark prevailed by just eighteen thousand votes, out of 4.5 million cast. It appeared that Democrats' electoral fortunes were about to rise along with their increasing share of registrants statewide.

That, however, proved not to be the case two years later, when a Democrat, Governor George Leader, was denied victory, largely by his own partisans in the southwestern part of the state who sought revenge against Leader for his attempts to reduce patronage. After his shocking defeat at the hands of Philadelphia congressman Hugh Scott, Leader would decide to never again run for office despite pleas from party leaders on more than one occasion. Scott would serve in the Senate for two more terms until his retirement, rising to the level of senate majority leader. His political skills were best demonstrated by his 1964 reelection, in which he narrowly defeated Genevieve Blatt, the state secretary of internal affairs, despite the fact that LBJ was carrying the state by 1.46 million votes. Clark, however, would not be so fortunate. After winning reelection, he was defeated in his quest for a third term by Congressman Richard Schweiker of Montgomery County. Again, Democratic defections were the culprit, especially in the Pittsburgh area, just as they had been with Leader and Blatt previously. It would not be until 2006 that the Democratic Party would win a full senate term in Pennsylvania.

The next major showdown occurred following Scott's retirement, pitting against each other two congressmen who were both viewed as rising stars in their party: Republican John Heinz of Pittsburgh and Democrat Bill Green of Philadelphia. In a contest in which geography played a role, many Democrats in the southwest once again defied their party and crossed over to vote for the GOP candidate. The Democrats would not even bother to offer a credible challenge to the popular and wealthy Heinz in any of his two reelection efforts. A battle did ensue following Schweiker's announcement that he was retiring from office and would not seek reelection in 1980 (he would later serve as secretary of health and human services in the Reagan Administration). Both parties offered candidates who had been defeated several times for statewide office. For the Republicans, it was Arlen Specter, a former district attorney who had tried and failed to win his party's nomination for US Senate in 1976 and for governor two years earlier, while the Democrats nominated Pete Flaherty, who had lost in the general elections for US Senate in 1974 and governor in 1978. Benefitting from Reagan's sweeping presidential victory, Specter won a close contest and, together with John Heinz, the state had two young ambitious senators. The Republicans seemingly had a vice grip on both seats for the foreseeable future.

That changed on April 4, 1991, when the 53-year-old Heinz was tragically killed along with six other people in a helicopter crash in Montgomery County. It was a shocking and devastating blow to the people of the state as they mourned the loss of their immensely popular public servant. Governor Casey, a Democrat, had the privilege of appointing a successor to fill out the rest of the late senator's term and, in a bit of a surprise, selected a member of his cabinet, Harris Wofford. Though he had a long history in the civil rights movement and had headed the Peace Corps during the Kennedy Administration, Wofford was somewhat unknown to the voters at large. In order to fill out the remaining three years of Heinz's term, he would need to win a special

Image 2.2 US Senator Hugh Scott with President Richard Nixon and Vice President Gerald Ford

Image 2.3 Future US Senator Arlen Specter with President Dwight D. Eisenhower

election in the fall of 1991, and when former governor and then-US Attorney General Richard Thornburgh announced his intention to challenge the appointed senator, the Democrat was viewed as a heavy underdog. However, in one of the most surprising upsets in the state's political history, Wofford, running a very aggressive campaign that focused on the need for national health care, shocked the political establishment by pulling off a relatively easy win.

With the election of President Bill Clinton the following year, there was much pressure on both the administration and Pennsylvania's newly elected senator to produce legislation on health care; in fact, Wofford was viewed to some degree as being responsible for putting it on the agenda. However, after that effort stalled in Congress, Wofford's approval ratings slid along with Clinton's, and the Democrat appeared more vulnerable than few would have imagined after his stunning win just three years earlier. His opponent was one-term congressman Rick Santorum of Allegheny County, a firebrand who was the most conservative candidate nominated by either party in well over a half century. Santorum's demeanor may have alienated some voters, but it was effective, at least this time, and he rode a huge GOP wave in 1994 right to the US Senate. For Democrats, however, it was another crushing defeat.

After winning reelection six years later, Santorum's popularity began to nosedive in his second term, and after the Democrats were able to convince their dream candidate, State Treasurer Robert Casey Jr., to challenge him, his career was essentially over. No matter what the incumbent attempted politically, the voters had made up their minds on the controversial senator, and the affable Casey, son of the former governor, defeated him by over seven hundred thousand votes. It was the second-largest defeat ever suffered by an incumbent senator in Pennsylvania, surpassed only by Democrat incumbent Joe Guffey's trouncing at the hands of Edward Martin back in 1946. It also marked the first time in forty-four years that a Democrat

Image 2.4 US Senator John Heinz

had won a regular six-year term in the Senate. Casey would go on to win reelection relatively easily in 2012; whether he can go on to be the first in his party to win three terms to the Senate remains to be seen.

As for the other senate seat, Arlen Specter would go on to win five consecutive terms, making him the longest-serving US senator in Pennsylvania's history. His closest call, in fact, came in the GOP primary, when he narrowly edged out a challenge from Lehigh Valley congressman Pat Toomey, who had support from the more conservative elements of the Republican Party. After surviving this close call, Specter, sensing that his more moderate positions on a number of issues left him increasingly vulnerable to a primary challenge, announced in April 2009 that he was, once again, a Democrat, switching back to the party he had belonged to when his career began in Philadelphia. It was also the first time that the Democrats held both of the state's senate seats since January 1947. Nevertheless, although the party establishment largely supported his reelection efforts, many others remembered vividly the battles that they had fought with Specter through his long career in office. He once again had to fight for his political career in a contested primary, this time to Delaware County congressman and former navy admiral Joe Sestak, who successfully attached his opponent to his previous record as a longtime Republican. After the bruising and costly primary, however, and facing a difficult national environment, Sestak narrowly lost in the fall to Pat Toomey, ironically the same individual who had forced Specter's party switch.

Image 2.5 US Senator Robert Casey, Jr.

With a presidential election year turnout facing him in 2016, it was expected that Toomey's reelection would be one of the nation's most anticipated and hard-fought contests, and it certainly did not disappoint. His Democratic opponent was Katie McGinty, a former environmental official at the national level under President Clinton and at the state level in the Rendell Administration. She had most recently served as Governor Wolf's chief of staff after losing to him in the Democratic primary in 2014. McGinty's candidacy was closely associated with Hillary Clinton's at the top of the Democratic ticket. Conventional wisdom leading up to Election Day suggested that McGinty's numbers would lag roughly 3–4 points behind Clinton, and with her candidate seemingly ahead throughout the campaign, it just became a question of how large Clinton's margin would be. Relative to this thinking, McGinty's performance proved better than expected; what proved shocking to many was how poorly Clinton ended up doing, eventually losing the state. Indeed, their numbers were almost identical to one another, with McGinty finishing just eighty-six thousand votes behind Toomey—less than a percentage point different from the Trump/Clinton margin. Had Clinton been able to generate a modicum of support in areas outside the southeastern part of the state, there is little doubt that McGinty would have been able to ride those coattails to the US Senate. Table 2.14 below lists each of the senators who have served the state since 1950, along with their home county and party affiliation.

UNITED STATES HOUSE OF REPRESENTATIVE ELECTIONS IN PENNSYLVANIA

As described in Table 2.15, the Democrats have possessed a majority within the Pennsylvania's congressional delegation for twenty terms since 1950, compared with 14 for the Republicans.

Table 2.14 Pennsylvania's United States Senators Since 1950

YEAR	SENATOR	PARTY	COUNTY	SENATOR	PARTY	COUNTY
1950				James Duff	Republican	Allegheny
1952	Edward Martin	Republican	Greene			
1956				Joe Clark	Democrat	Philadelphia
1958	Hugh Scott	Republican	Philadelphia			
1962				Joe Clark	Democrat	Philadelphia
1964	Hugh Scott	Republican	Philadelphia			
1968				Richard Schweiker	Republican	Montgomery
1970	Hugh Scott	Republican	Philadelphia			
1974				Richard Schweiker	Republican	Montgomery
1976	John Heinz	Republican	Allegheny			

(Continued)

Table 2.14 (*Continued*)

YEAR	SENATOR	PARTY	COUNTY	SENATOR	PARTY	COUNTY
1980				Arlen Specter	Republican	Philadelphia
1982	John Heinz	Republican	Allegheny			
1986				Arlen Specter	Republican	Philadelphia
1988	John Heinz	Republican	Allegheny			
199*	Harris Wofford	Democrat	Montgomery			
1992				Arlen Specter	Republican	Philadelphia
1994	Rick Santorum	Republican	Allegheny			
1998				Arlen Specter	Republican	Philadelphia
2000	Rick Santorum	Republican	Allegheny			
2004				Arlen Specter	Republican	Philadelphia
2006	Robert Casey Jr.	Democrat	Lackawanna			
2010				Pat Toomey	Republican	Lehigh
2012	Robert Casey Jr.	Democrat	Lackawanna			
2016				Pat Toomey	Republican	Lehigh

Note: Senator Specter is listed as a Republican, which was his party affiliation at the time of his last election. He later switched to the Democratic party during that term.

While the GOP has dominated the states' delegation in recent years they still have a long way to go before they can match the Democrats streak of control for thirteen congresses running from 1964-1990. However, the 13-5 advantage held by the Republicans over the last three electoral cycles outpaces anything either party has accomplished during this period. Their support stems largely from the results of the 2010 election, one in which the GOP routed the Democrats nationally in what was President Barack Obama's first midterm. As a result, the Republicans took control of the Pennsylvania delegation as well as the majority in the chamber overall after picking up sixty-three house seats across the nation, the biggest swing since 1948 and the largest in a midterm since 1938.

However, the impact of this was widespread as it came during the election cycle on the precipice of a new national census and subsequent redistricting. The end results is that with the Republicans in control both houses of the Pennsylvania General Assembly as well as the Governor's office with the victory by Tom Corbett that same year, the GOP was able to redraw the legislative lines across the Commonwealth which would only expand their opportunities going forward (the issue of redistricting is more thoroughly discussed in Chapter Four). How creative was this gerrymander? Following the 2012 election, Democratic candidates for the United States House of Representatives tallied 52 percent of the aggregate statewide vote. However, this netted them only 5 of the 18 seats overall!

Table 2.15 Partisan Distribution of Seats in Pennsylvania's Congressional Delegation

YEAR	NUMBER OF DISTRICTS	DEMOCRATIC SEATS	REPUBLICAN SEATS
1950	33	13	20
1952	30	11	19
1954	30	14	16
1956	30	13	17
1958	30	16	14
1960	30	14	16
1962	27	13	14
1964	27	15	12
1966	27	14	13
1968	27	14	13
1970	27	14	13
1972	25	13	12
1974	25	14	11
1976	25	17	8
1978	25	15	10
1980	25	13	12
1982	23	13	10
1984	23	13	10
1986	23	12	11
1988	23	12	11
1990	23	11	12
1992	21	11	10
1994	21	11	10
1996	21	11	10
1998	21	11	10
2000	21	10	11
2002	19	7	12
2004	19	7	12
2006	19	11	8
2008	19	12	7
2010	19	7	12
2012	18	5	13
2014	18	5	13
2016	18	5	13
Delegation Control	Republicans 18 Terms	Democrats 16 Terms	

Source: *The Pennsylvania Manual*.

Republicans had a similar opportunity to gerrymander following the 2000 and certainly did so, enhancing their edge in the delegation from 11-10 to 12-7, However, they miscalculated both changing voting patterns as well as how resilient some of their representatives were and left some of the margins much too thin. Subsequently, facing a rough environment in 2006 during President George W. Bush's second midterm a number of these seats were washed away and the Democrats now had a majority, at least temporarily. Half-way through this redistricting, there is no evidence that GOP map drawers made the same mistake twice. It would take a wave election of historical proportions to propel the Democrats to a majority until the next maps are implemented for the 2022 elections.

STATE ROW OFFICE ELECTIONS IN PENNSYLVANIA

There are currently three elected row offices in Pennsylvania: attorney general, state treasurer, and auditor-general. Attorney general, generally considered the highest of the three in power and prestige, became an elected office for the first time in 1980. Also, two other offices, lieutenant governor and internal affairs, were independent elected offices prior to a revision at the 1968 state constitutional convention. At that time, lieutenant governor was merged as part of a team ticket elected together with the governor. The Office of Internal Affairs was abolished entirely, and its main responsibilities were shifted to the Department of State, which is located in the executive branch, and a secretary, who is appointed by the governor. Both of these offices have been excluded from this table. Additionally, prior to another change at the convention, individuals elected to serve in these offices were limited to one term, the same limitation placed upon governors. Beginning with the 1970 contests, they have been eligible to serve for two terms. It should be noted that each of these positions is examined in more detail, particularly as it relates to their responsibilities, in Chapter Five.

Republicans have dominated the races for state attorney general since it first became an elective office, prevailing in eight of the ten contests, though the Democrats have won the last two (Table 2.16). Twice previously, Democrats came extraordinarily close to finally breaking through. Both Joe Kohn in 1996 and Jim Eisenhower in 2004 were even declared the winners by some news outlets, only to see their leads disappear in the early morning hours. In fact, each of the Democratic candidates, except for those in the 2000 and 2008 contests, were within three percentage points away from victory. Voters overall seemed to prefer the crime-fighting focus that Republicans tended to emphasize rather than the more active role in regulating consumer interests that the Democrats more often highlighted. However, when the party finally broke through behind Kathleen Kane in 2012, they did it in grand fashion, rolling up an 800,000-vote margin as she became

Image 2.6 Former State Attorney General Kathleen Kane

Table 2.16 Pennsylvania's Elected Attorneys General Since 1980

YEAR	OFFICE HOLDER	PARTY
1980	Leroy Zimmerman	Republican
1984	Leroy Zimmerman	Republican
1988	Ernie Preate	Republican
1992	Ernie Preate	Republican
1996	Mike Fisher	Republican
2000	Mike Fisher	Republican
2004	Tom Corbett	Republican
2008	Tom Corbett	Republican
2012	Kathleen Kane	Democrat
2016	Josh Shapiro	Democrat
Victories	Republicans 8 Democrats 2	

not only the first Democrat to be elected to the post but also the first woman. Her meteoric rise made Kane the political story of the year, and she was ticketed for even higher office immediately. However, after a successful beginning in the office, she found herself at the center of a number of controversies: whether she had leaked grand jury testimony illegally to the press; that she failed to prosecute several Democratic state representatives from Philadelphia for alleged corruption; and being at the center of what would become known as "Porngate," a scandal involving whether a number of prominent officeholders, including several members of the state supreme court, were downloading and sending obscene materials on their state-owned computers. In February

US Senator Pat Toomey at Budget Committee Hearing

Table 2.17 Pennsylvania's Elected State Treasurers Since 1950

YEAR	OFFICEHOLDER	PARTY
1952	Weldon Heyburn	Republican
1956	Robert Kent	Republican
1960	Grace Sloan	Democrat
1964	Tom Minehart	Democrat
1968	Grace Sloan	Democrat
1972	Grace Sloan	Democrat
1976	Robert E. Casey	Democrat
1980	R. Budd Dwyer	Republican
1984	R. Budd Dwyer	Republican
1988	Catherine B. Knoll	Democrat
1992	Catherine B. Knoll	Democrat
1996	Barbara Hafer	Republican
2000	Barbara Hafer	Republican
2004	Robert Casey Jr.	Democrat
2008	Rob McCord	Democrat
2012	Rob McCord	Democrat
2016	Joe Torsella	Democrat
Victories	Democrats 11 Republicans 6	

2016, facing a continuing barrage of both legal and political charges as well as several primary challengers, she announced that she would not seek reelection. It was as dramatic an ending to a political career as was her rise in the beginning.

Democrats were able to hold the office when former state representative and current Montgomery county commissioner Josh Shapiro defeated State Senator John Rafferty, also of Montgomery County, by roughly three percentage points. Shapiro, who was for many the party's top choice to challenge Senator Toomey for his seat, instead set his sights on this statewide office, perhaps as a stepping stone to one day run for governor, with perhaps an eye on succeeding Wolf.

In the other two offices, Democrats have had the advantage, winning eleven and thirteen of the sixteen races for treasurer (Table 2.17) and auditor-general (Table 2.18), respectively. What is surely particularly concerning regarding each of these races is the impact that the presidential contests at the top of the ballot have upon them. Democrats have captured the last four for treasurer and the last six for auditor-general and, with attorney general, swept all

Table 2.18 Pennsylvania Auditors-General Since 1950

YEAR	OFFICEHOLDER	PARTY
1952	Charles Barber	Republican
1956	Charles Smith	Republican
1960	Tom Minehart	Democrat
1964	Grace Sloan	Democrat
1968	Robert P. Casey	Democrat
1972	Robert P. Casey	Democrat
1976	Al Benedict	Democrat
1980	Al Benedict	Democrat
1984	Don Bailey	Democrat
1988	Barbara Hafer	Republican
1992	Barbara Hafer	Republican
1996	Robert Casey Jr.	Democrat
2000	Robert Casey Jr.	Democrat
2004	Jack Wagner	Democrat
2008	Jack Wagner	Democrat
2012	Gene DePasquale	Democrat
2014	Gene DePasquale	Democrat
Victories	Democrats 13 Republicans 4	

three in both 2012 and 2016. Again, this demonstrates the advantage that the Democrats have at the macro level of state politics but, as we will soon see, is absent at the microlegislative level.

STATE LEGISLATIVE ELECTIONS IN PENNSYLVANIA

As Table 2.19 illustrates, control of the Pennsylvania House of Representatives has been as closely contested as it could possibly be since 1950, with the Republicans in the majority for eighteen terms and their Democratic rivals for sixteen. However, while the Democrats tended to do better prior to the 1990s (and in particular the stretch between the 1982 and 1994 elections, in which they controlled every session), the Republicans have been more successful ever since. Except for the four-year period which began following the 2006 election, the GOP has maintained control throughout, and its total number of members today, 121, is the largest their

Table 2.19 Partisan Breakdown of the Pennsylvania House of Representatives

YEAR	DEMOCRATS	REPUBLICANS	MAJORITY
1950	87	120	Republican
1952	98	110	Republican
1954	112	98	Democrats
1956	83	126	Republican
1958	108	102	Democrats
1960	109	101	Democrats
1962	98	108	Republican
1964	116	93	Democrats
1966	99	103	Republican
1968	106	96	Democrats
1970	112	90	Democrats
1972	95	108	Republican
1974	114	89	Democrats
1976	118	84	Democrats
1978	100	103	Republican
1980	100	102	Republican
1982	103	100	Democrats
1984	103	100	Democrats
1986	101	100	Democrats
1988	103	99	Democrats
1990	107	96	Democrats
1992	102	97	Democrats
1994	100	102	Republican
1996	99	103	Republican
1998	100	103	Republican
2000	97	103	Republican
2002	94	105	Republican
2004	93	109	Republican
2006	102	101	Democrats
2008	104	97	Democrats
2010	91	112	Republican
2012	90	111	Republican
2014	84	119	Republican
2016	82	121	Republican
Victories	Republicans 18 Terms	Democrats 16 Terms	

Source: *The Pennsylvania Manual.*

delegation has been since the election following the 1956 election, when President Eisenhower was running for reelection.

In the state senate, however, the GOP has been truly dominant throughout the period of this study, maintaining control of the upper house the entire time save for the decade of the 1970s, when the Democrats grabbed control and kept it through five election cycles (Table 2.20). However, since another Republican president, this time Ronald Reagan, led the ticket in 1980, they have remarkably maintained control throughout, especially given that their Democratic rivals have benefited from having more registered voters during this entire time. In all, the Republicans have controlled the state senate in twenty-eight of the legislative terms since 1950, while the Democrats lag behind at five. The legislative session following the 1960 election ended in a 25–25 split in the Senate.

The Republicans have had complete control of both branches in the General Assembly for fourteen of the last thirty-four legislative sessions, which includes the last four and ten of the last twelve. Their Democratic counterparts have had sole control only three times, following the 1970, 1974, and 1976 elections. Additionally, it should be noted that Republicans had a vice grip on legislative control long before this study began in 1950. Prior to 1954, when the

Table 2.20 Partisan Breakdown of the Pennsylvania Senate

YEAR	DEMOCRATS	REPUBLICANS	MAJORITY
1950	20	30	Republican
1952	18	32	Republican
1954	24	26	Republican
1956	23	27	Republican
1958	22	28	Republican
1960	25	25	Tie
1962	22	26	Republican
1964	22	27	Republican
1966	22	27	Republican
1968	23	27	Republican
1970	25	24	Democrats
1972	27	24	Democrats
1974	30	20	Democrats
1976	30	20	Democrats
1978	28	22	Democrats
1980	24	26	Republican
1982	23	27	Republican
1984	23	27	Republican
1986	24	26	Republican

(Continued)

Table 2.20 (*Continued*)

YEAR	DEMOCRATS	REPUBLICANS	MAJORITY
1988	23	27	Republican
1990	24	26	Republican
1992	24	26	Republican
1994	21	27	Republican
1996	20	30	Republican
1998	20	30	Republican
2000	20	29	Republican
2002	21	29	Republican
2004	21	28	Republican
2006	21	29	Republican
2008	19	30	Republican
2010	19	30	Republican
2012	23	27	Republican
2014	20	30	Republican
2016	16	34	Republican
Victories	Republicans 28 Terms	Democrats 5 Terms	Tie 1

Source: *The Pennsylvania Manual*. Note: For both the house and senate numbers, at times the figures do not add up 203 and 50 seats, respectively. This is due to vacancies, and in addition, there were instances in which special elections changed the breakdown within a session. In those cases, the number used were those immediately following the election.

Democrats seized the House of Representatives, one would need to go back to the 1940 election to find a cycle that left them in control. For the Senate, the drought was even longer: prior to the 1970 election (and except for the one tie in 1960), Democrats last captured this body in the 1960 elections.

VOTER TURNOUT IN PENNSYLVANIA ELECTIONS

Lastly, Pennsylvania historically tended to rank below the national average as it pertains to Election Day turnout. However, that seems to be changing somewhat. Since comprehensive data first became available beginning in 1980 and continuing until the 2002 cycle, only once, in 1986, was the state turnout higher, and in that case, it was very modest (Table 2.21). However, since that time, voters have been more likely to participate, and the state has been slightly above the mean nationally.

A number of factors influence turnout levels in a particular state, one of which is the location itself. The state's individualistic culture, as mentioned in Chapter One, is not as conducive to higher turnout as the moralistic culture, but it is a better environment than that found in states with traditionalist cultures. Higher levels of education and socioeconomic status

Table 2.21 Voter Turnout in Pennsylvania Compared with the National Average

YEAR		VEP		VEP	DIFFERENCE
2016	United States	60.2%	Pennsylvania	63.0%	2.8
2014	United States	36.0%	Pennsylvania	36.1%	0.1
2012	United States	58.0%	Pennsylvania	59.5%	1.5
2010	United States	41.0%	Pennsylvania	41.7%	0.7
2008	United States	61.6%	Pennsylvania	63.6%	2
2006	United States	40.4%	Pennsylvania	44.1%	3.7
2004	United States	60.1%	Pennsylvania	62.6%	2.6
2002	United States	39.5%	Pennsylvania	38.8%	-0.6
2000	United States	54.2%	Pennsylvania	54.1%	-0.1
1998	United States	38.1%	Pennsylvania	33.3%	-4.8
1996	United States	51.7%	Pennsylvania	49.7%	-2
1994	United States	41.1%	Pennsylvania	39.6%	-1.5
1992	United States	58.1%	Pennsylvania	54.9%	-3.2
1990	United States	38.4%	Pennsylvania	34.1%	-4.3
1988	United States	52.8%	Pennsylvania	51.0%	-1.8
1986	United States	38.1%	Pennsylvania	38.4%	0.3
1984	United States	55.2%	Pennsylvania	55.1%	-0.1
1982	United States	42.1%	Pennsylvania	42.1%	0
1980	United States	54.2%	Pennsylvania	52.6%	-1.6

Source: US Election Project. Note: Voter Eligible Population is chosen as a comparative method rather than the Voting Age Population due to the fact that the ineligible population varies widely across the nation due to differing laws within each state relative to those with criminal convictions. In Pennsylvania, those on probation or parole are eligible while in other states they are not. Conversely, in two states, Vermont and Maine, those actually incarcerated are eligible.

are also indicators, and the state hovers right around the middle nationwide. According to United States Census Data, Pennsylvania ranks twenty-fourth in the percentage of high school graduates, twenty-fifth in the percentage of those with a college degree, and slightly better than average in those with an advanced degree (nineteenth). As for socioeconomic indicators, the state places twenty-third in median household income and nineteenth in per capita income.

However, there are several factors present in Pennsylvania's environment that might contribute in a positive fashion to the state's turnout. For instance, since older citizens are more likely to participate than younger ones, Pennsylvania's median household age of 40.10, which places it sixth nationally, should be expected to have a net positive effect. In addition, the state is still considered competitive both nationally and in most statewide elections, and that combination, along with strong parties more than willing to invest time and money in get-out-the-vote efforts, should also support strong turnout.

However, in recent years, many states have reformed their voting procedures, allowing such mechanisms as early voting, same-day registration, and even voting by mail. In Pennsylvania, however, officials have been slow to change their procedures; even efforts such as Governor Rendell's efforts to move up the presidential primary in the state so that it could be more relative to the national system have fallen short. As always, citizens must be registered within thirty days of any election in order to vote.

One final factor, which impacts voting in selecting party nominees, is the closed primary system that Pennsylvania continues to employ. It is one of nine states that use this method, in which those not registered with a particular party cannot vote in their primaries; in other words, only Democrats may vote in that party's primary and likewise for Republicans. It is one reason why the number of unaffiliated voters in the state is relatively low, since individuals registering this way are frozen out of the process in selecting candidates. It should be noted that in one-party regions, such as a county like Philadelphia for the Democrats or Lancaster County for the GOP, in many respects the real competition is in the spring—with the winner almost certainly prevailing in the fall. The state's strong two parties themselves also support this system, since there is less uncertainty in the electorate and the party has a stronger grip on the process, especially through issuing their endorsements. Opponents charge that, by excluding more independently minded citizens from participating in the selection of candidates, it has helped contribute to the greater polarization that has developed in our political system, with the two ideological extremes dominating.

In contrast, there are also fourteen states that have truly open primaries, allowing any registered voter to participate in the selection of a party's candidate regardless of their own individual political affiliation (Table 2.22). An open primary not only allows unaffiliated voters to choose either party's primary; it also allows registered Democrats to cross over and vote in the Republican primary (and vice versa). While supporters argue that this is more democratic and inclusive, opponents counter that it interferes with a particular party's ability to nominate its own preferred candidate. It also makes a party vulnerable to "raiding," a process by which individuals cross over to vote for the candidate of the opposition party they believe will be most vulnerable in the general election. There is anecdotal evidence that this has occurred at the margins in presidential campaigns when voters crossed over to make mischief with the other's nomination process after their party choice had been defined.

A number of states also use a hybrid-type system. In a semiclosed primary, found in eleven states, unaffiliated voters can participate in either party's primary; however, those registered with a party are unable to cross over. There are even differences within semiclosed primaries: some allow Independents to make their selections privately in the voting booth, while others demand that the Independent voter actually register with that particular party on Election Day.

Table 2.22 State Primary System by Type

CLOSED (9)	SEMICLOSED (11)	SEMIOPEN (13)	OPEN (14)	BLANKET (3)
Delaware	Alabama	Alaska	Connecticut	California
Florida	Arkansas	Arizona	Idaho	Louisiana
Kentucky	Georgia	Colorado	Illinois	Washington
Maine	Hawaii	Indiana	Maryland	
Nevada	Michigan	Iowa	Mississippi	
New Jersey	Minnesota	Kansas	Nebraska	
New Mexico	Missouri	Massachusetts	Ohio	
New York	Montana	New Hampshire	Oklahoma	
Pennsylvania	North Dakota	North Carolina	Oregon	
	Vermont	Rhode Island	South Carolina	
	Wisconsin	Utah	South Dakota	
		West Virginia	Tennessee	
		Wyoming	Texas	
			Virginia	

Source: Data provided by the National Council of State Legislatures.

Additionally, there are thirteen states that utilize what is known as a semiopen primary. In this system, a registered voter is able to vote in either party's primary; however, they must declare publicly which one they will be voting in. This decision is marked by a poll worker, and the individual voter is given a party specific ballot.

The fifth type of candidate-selection system used nationwide is known as either a blanket or two-tiered primary. In this system, generally used by three states, all candidates are listed together on one ballot, regardless of party affiliation, and the top two vote-getters advance to the general election. This system has the potential for pitting two candidates of the same party against each other in a general election, a scenario that occurred in 2012 when Democratic Congressman Brad Sherman defeated another Democrat, Howard Berman, after their two legislative districts were combined following the 2000 census. It should be noted that one other state, Nebraska, uses this only for its nonpartisan legislative elections. Additionally, no state uses this option for the presidential selection process.

3 THE PENNSYLVANIA CONSTITUTION

Put forward by William Penn, the initial constitution (entitled The Frame of Government of Pennsylvania) of the state named in his honor created a unicameral legislature that predated the United States House of Representatives by 107 years. It ranks as one of the oldest remaining legislative bodies on Earth. Later, in three successive frames of government (adopted in 1683, 1696, and 1701), the general outlines of Pennsylvania's colonial government were cemented. Each of the four frames established a government with three branches—legislative, executive, and judicial—built to check one another. Each was also consistent with the Lockean ideals of governments requiring the consent of the people and indirect rather than direct democracy. Additionally, governmental authority in each frame was limited to what was expressed in the written articles.[21]

The final frame, entitled The Charter of Privileges Granted by William Penn, Esquire, to the Inhabitants of Pennsylvania and Territories, gave the assembly the ability to choose its own officers, set its own adjournments, appoint committees, and pass laws. Established as an independent body, the assembly, via this treatise, would govern the colony until the signing of the Declaration of Independence in 1776.[22]

THE CONSTITUTION OF 1776

In response to the Declaration of Independence and the request of the Second Continental Congress to the colonies to reject British rule, the Pennsylvania's state constitutional convention began in June 1776. Led by Benjamin Franklin and influenced by the ideas of noted French philosopher Jean-Jacques Rousseau, the result was an idealistic treatise that emphasized the maximum participation of the citizenry. Containing the Declaration of the Rights of the Inhabitants of the Commonwealth, or State of Pennsylvania, it is regarded as the most democratic in America at that time. The constitution also provided Pennsylvania with its official title as that of a commonwealth.

Under this new constitution, the first established within the now-independent nation, the requirement that citizens own property in order to vote and hold public office was abolished, and suffrage was extended to include all men who paid taxes. The Quaker philosophy regarding religious freedom also persisted, stipulating that no "man who acknowledges the being of a God (may) be justly deprived or abridged of any civil right as a citizen." Due process was also inscribed, as was the ability of individuals to buy their release from military service.

Pennsylvania also preserved the unicameral legislature, referred to as the House of Representatives or the General Assembly, which was established during the colonial period and was unique among the states. A senate, looked upon by these French-influenced leaders as just another version of the British House of Lords, was absent. They felt that the will of the people could best be wielded through a single chamber. Also, as in the provincial assembly, representatives to the House were elected annually and could not serve for more than "four years in seven years." Annual sessions were stipulated, although there was no provision for calling special sessions. Constraints on lawmaking itself were imposed, as no bill could be enacted until one year from the time it was formally read and printed. Additionally, there was no provision for a governor (who was viewed as a new form of a king), and the judiciary lacked any degree of independence. Judges, whose terms lasted just seven years, could be removed at any time by the legislature for "misbehavior."[23] All of these features combined to give Pennsylvania the most politically bold and audacious document yet conceived by any of the new states.

However, these democratic precepts were not without their critics, both from inside and outside Pennsylvania's borders. To them, it was far too radical. For example, Federalists, with their beliefs in a powerful government, simply despised these French-inspired democratic ideals at first sight. Also, many in the business community firmly believed that this rotation inspired political uncertainty, which in turn would negatively impact commerce. Ultimately, opposition intensified to the point that a decision to replace it was finally made fourteen years later with a document that would shift the focus of power in the other direction.

THE CONSTITUTION OF 1790

"The legislative power of this commonwealth shall be vested in a General Assembly, which shall consist of a Senate and a House of Representatives." With this statement from the Constitution of 1790, the Pennsylvania legislature—obviously influenced by the recently approved Constitution of the United States, became a bicameral body.

Although the legislature was to determine the size of each house, the constitution established several basic guidelines. The House could have between sixty and one hundred members, while the size of the Senate would fall between one-third and one-fourth the size of the House. The allocation of seats in the House was to be based on the number of taxable inhabitants, with each existing county entitled to at least one representative. Newly created counties would receive no representation until their numbers reached the established ratio. Senate districts were based on the number of taxable inhabitants in each region, limited to no more than four individual seats. The terms of office were also set: one year for the House, four years for the Senate.

The establishment of a formal chief executive ("The supreme executive power of this commonwealth shall be vested in a governor") also substantively changed the nature of the state's system. In many respects, the qualifications and powers, including the ability to appoint officials within the executive branch of government, reflect those given to the president of the United States in the recently ratified US Constitution; they even provide a reservoir of power not previously imagined under the original constitution with the statement that "he shall take care that the laws be faithfully executed."

THE CONSTITUTION OF 1838

Unlike the first two constitutions, the Constitution of 1838 offered little fundamental change to Pennsylvania's basic governmental structure. However, its biggest impact was to alter the relationship between the executive and legislative branches, largely at the expense of the former. The thrust of this convention (the first convened at the behest of a popular referendum) was an overall distrust of the executive branch, which the delegates further weakened by taking away some degree of the governor's appointment powers. It took away the power of the governor to appoint local officials and gave the Senate a stake in appointing judges. The judicial branch was impacted as well, as life tenure was eliminated in favor of a fifteen-year term.

Also, it contained a provision, which still remains in effect, for amendment of single sections of the Pennsylvania Constitution. This served as the legal basis later in 1857 for additional changes to the legislature via the amendment process. Senate terms were reduced to three years, and although the House remained unchanged, several stipulations affected its election procedures. For instance, representatives were to be apportioned by dividing the number of taxable inhabitants by one hundred (the disenfranchisement of black citizens would continue). Also, the protection of smaller counties was cemented when it was established that no more than three counties could be joined and no county could be divided to form a district.[24]

The net effect of this constitution was to swing the legislative/executive pendulum back towards the former's side, though certainly not to where it rested after the initial constitution.

THE CONSTITUTION OF 1874

With the fever of anticorruption reform sweeping the nation, Pennsylvanians again gathered to change the state's constitution. A growing sense of distrust and disillusionment prevailed, which led to calls for the imposition of tighter restrictions on both legislative and executive powers.

Ultimately, the state's fourth constitution would have a profound impact on Pennsylvania government in general and on the legislature specifically. The structure of today's legislature is largely a product of this document. Terms of office in the House of Representatives were changed from one year to two, and the Senate was moved back to a four-year term. These rules are still in effect. The House of Representatives was enlarged to two hundred members, and the Senate was fixed at fifty. The reapportionment of seats in the legislature would take place after each United States decennial census. A growing population base also demanded a change in the basic formula that determined the allocation of legislative districts. The ratio was increased in the House by dividing the population by two hundred and continuing to give each county at least one representative while allowing no district more than four. In the Senate, no county could have representation greater than one-sixth of the total number of senators. The ratio in the Senate would be determined by dividing the population by fifty.[25]

Other notable changes were brought forward by the Constitution of 1874. The office of lieutenant governor and the Department of Internal Affairs were created. The constitution also provided for the popular election of judges, the state treasurer, and the auditor-general. Although the governor's term was expanded from three to four years, governors were no longer permitted to succeed themselves. The legislative power of the governor was enhanced when the office was given the power to veto line items in appropriation bills. A two-thirds vote in both houses was required to override any executive veto. For nearly a century, the Constitution of 1874 was the commonwealth's governing document.

THE CONSTITUTION OF 1968

A number of states have clauses in their constitutions requiring that conventions be called during specific time periods. In fact, five states (AL, HA, IA, NH, and RI) force the issue to be addressed within as short a time period as every ten years. Several others require it as well, albeit within a longer interval. Most states, however, allow conventions to be called either through the citizen-petition route or with a majority or supermajority of the legislature. Interestingly, Pennsylvania is one of the few states in which no constitutional option specifically mentions providing for a new convention. Nevertheless, that hasn't prevented the state from having five of them anyway, with the most recent one occurring in 1968, when the current constitution was adopted. Rather than explicit constitutional authorization, the state legislature approached it as a manner of tradition (and there was precedent) and put the question on the ballot for the voters to decide.

The process began as early as 1961, when future governor Milton J. Shapp led the Committee for State Constitutional Revision in forcing the legislature to call for a referendum on the subject. In early 1967, the legislature passed a bill enabling a constitutional convention, which would leave it to the state's electorate to decide. Subsequently approved by the voters during the 1967 primary, the constitutional convention (or "Con-Con," as it was called) began in earnest on December 1, 1967, when its secretary, noted author James A. Michener, called the proceedings to order. The 163 delegates who attended the convention were divided roughly along partisan lines, with eighty-eight Republicans and seventy-five Democrats.

Since the delegates were limited to amending four areas of the former constitution (judiciary, state finance, local government, and legislative reapportionment), overall change was bound to be incremental. Furthermore, the delegates were prevented from altering the constitution's uniformity clause, which prohibited a graduated income tax. Ultimately, five issues were agreed upon, and the corresponding questions were placed on the ballot during the 1968 primary election. These referenda included (1) judicial questions, such as the creation of a new commonwealth court and merit retention of statewide judges; (2) guarantee of home rule for all units of local government; (3) limits on state borrowing and the requirement that the budget shall be balanced; and (4) that certain tax exemptions, particularly those affecting the poor, would be permitted. The fifth main change in the state's constitution involved the legislature itself when it was agreed upon to finally establish a specific number for the size of each chamber, a decision that will be examined in more detail in Chapter Three.

Although the 1968 convention had little impact on the overall makeup of the legislature, significant changes were created by other sources. In the elections of 1966–67, voters, for the first time, approved the measure that would make the General Assembly a two-year, continuously meeting body. Of further significance were the results of the 1966 reapportionment, which eliminated all multimember districts from the House. In the 1965–66 legislative session, the last to have multiple-county districts, ninety-three members came from such districts.

However, while the elimination of multimember districts had an obvious impact on the state's politicians and mapmakers, its overall impact on politics has perhaps been minimal. According to political scientist Frank Sorauf, who examined Pennsylvania in his book *Party and Representation*:

> Only once since the 1953 apportionment has a candidate been elected in a multiple-member district with less than a majority vote. The Eisenhower landslide of 1956 carried to office a Republican from Northampton County with a 49.4 percent vote. Clearly, then, a strong party system capable of maintaining cohesive voting for its candidates in multiple-member districts—and Pennsylvania appears to have it—can forestall the representational quirks and distortions that these districts might otherwise introduce.[26]

Another important change affecting the legislature was a decision by the Pennsylvania Supreme Court to abolish the requirement that each of the state's sixty-seven counties have its own house seat. This change was based on the "one man, one vote" principle established a few years earlier by the United States Supreme Court in the landmark *Baker v. Carr* (1962) and *Reynolds v. Sims* (1964) cases. Consequently, a degree of political power shifted from the sparsely populated rural counties, which were now unable to meet the population criteria necessary to justify their own legislative seats. In sum, a total of ten counties, concentrated in the north central part of the state, were left without their own individual representatives. Thus, reapportionment created, for the first time, legislative districts that divided individual counties. Similarly, the application of the "one man, one vote" principle effectively killed a provision of the state's constitution stipulating that no county could have more than one-sixth of the seats in the state senate. This reduction in the power of rural regions did not, however, significantly increase the numbers or power of any other area. For example, Philadelphia County, which had a total of thirty-five representatives, remained unchanged, while Allegheny County had an increase of only one seat. Thus, the net result of reapportionment was simply to lower the number of seats in the General Assembly from 209 to 203 rather than truly altering its geographic makeup. Additionally, the General Assembly of 1967 held the distinction of being the first to assign statewide district numbers.

THE FEATURES OF PENNSYLVANIA'S CONSTITUTION

The majority of state constitutions are quite long, especially when compared to the Constitution of the United States, which contains 7,652 words (including the twenty-seven amendments that have since been added). The shortest of the state constitutions is that of Vermont, which contains 8,419 words, and the longest is Louisiana's, with 184,053 words. The number of words in Pennsylvania's current constitution, including amendments, is 25,878, slightly less than the overall average of about 27,000.

Several reasons have been cited for why state constitutions are lengthier than their federal counterpart, but fundamentally, it is because the framers limited the federal government by design, and a brief, concise document outlining the powers possessed by the national government reflected this fact. Recall that it was written in an environment in which the existing government, the Articles of Confederation, was a state-centered system that provided little power to the national government.

Another factor contributing to the size of state constitutions (particularly those created after 1900, after which constitutions tended to be much longer) was the general distrust many political elites held for state legislatures. Also, many states allow amendments to their constitutions to be brought by citizens through the initiative process, which has cluttered many with items that could be better handled through simple laws.

Pennsylvania's constitutional structure does follow the typical format by beginning with a preamble, following with a bill of rights and the enumeration of the three branches of government, continuing with items related to election procedures, taxation, and local government powers, and finishing with the process prescribed to amend the document. This is typical of state constitutions as they reflect the basic structure of the United States Constitution. The preamble states, "We, the people of the Commonwealth of Pennsylvania, grateful to Almighty

God for the blessings of civil and religious liberty, humbly invoking His guidance, do ordain and establish this Constitution." The structure of the constitution is as follows:

Table 3.1 Organization of the Pennsylvania Constitution

PREAMBLE	
Article I:	Declaration of Rights
Article II:	The Legislature
Article III:	Legislation
Article IV:	The Executive
Article V:	The Judiciary
Article VI:	Public Officers
Article VII:	Elections
Article VIII:	Taxation and Finance
Article IX:	Local Government
Article X:	Private Corporations
Article XI:	Amendments

Article I: Declaration of Rights

There are twenty-eight sections contained within Article I, which outlines the basic rights that the citizens of Pennsylvania possess. It includes political rights, stipulating that the people "have at all times an inalienable and indefeasible right to alter, reform, or abolish their government in such manner as they may think proper." Political rights are also contained in another section on elections, which ensures that "elections shall be free and equal; and no power, civil or military, shall at any time interfere to prevent the free exercise of the right of suffrage."

Given the state's Quaker origins, of course it is not surprising that religious rights are also prominently mentioned towards the opening of Article I, stipulating that "all men have a natural and indefeasible right to worship Almighty God according to their dictates" and continuing with "no preference shall ever be given by law to any religious establishments or modes of worship."

Much like the middle section of the US Constitution's Bill of Rights, Article I of the Pennsylvania Constitution also lays out some of the basic tenets of its judicial system as well as the fundamental rights possessed by those criminally accused. Among these are trial by jury; protections from unreasonable searches and seizures; protection from double jeopardy; eminent domain; and the prohibition of excessive bail, fines, and punishment. Also included are freedoms of the press and speech.

In addition, Article I reflects the national constitution in granting its citizens the right to bear arms as well as protection against the forcible quartering of soldiers, much like the former's Second and Third Amendments.

Article II: The Legislature

The legislature is the first branch of government defined in the Pennsylvania Constitution. The Pennsylvania legislature's bicameral nature is like that of every other state save Nebraska, with fifty senators elected to four-year terms (one-half are elected every two years) and 203 House members holding two-year terms. However, unlike a number of other states, Pennsylvania's General Assembly is a body that continually meets and can legislate at any time during a lawmaker's term of office.

The age requirement for members of the Senate is twenty-five years, and for the House of Representatives, it is twenty-one. To be qualified for legislative office, individuals must also be citizens and inhabitants of the state for four years, reside in their districts one year prior to their elections, and must maintain residence within such district during their terms of service.

The geographic qualities of legislative districts are also mentioned in Article II. In particular, a passage that reads "unless absolutely necessary, no county, city, incorporated town, borough, township, or ward shall be divided in forming either a senatorial or representative district" served as the basis for Pennsylvania's supreme court in January 2012 to throw out the maps drawn by the Legislative Reapportionment Commission.

The Legislative Reapportionment Commission itself is outlined in the legislative article, establishing a five-member commission. Four of the members include the majority and minority leaders of the Senate and the House. The all-important fifth person, in effect the tiebreaker, is selected by the others. If no one can be agreed upon, the final decision is left to a majority selection by the seven-member Pennsylvania Supreme Court.

Lastly, senators and representatives are prohibited from being appointed to any civil office in the commonwealth that provides for a salary, nor can a member simultaneously be a member of the United States Congress while serving in the General Assembly. In all, the legislative article consists of seventeen sections.

Article III: Legislation

Specifics relating to the legislative process are provided their own article, which consists of thirty-two specific sections. Many of these relate to the internal operating procedures of the General Assembly, such as committee requirements, notice and signing of bills, and the amendment process. There are important additional subitems covered, however, such as the National Guard (maintained by the GA, also allowing for conscientious objector status for bearing arms) and education. Two important passages regarding the latter stipulate that "the General Assembly shall provide for the maintenance and support of a thorough and efficient system of public education" and "no money raised for the support of the public schools of the Commonwealth shall be appropriated to or used for the support of a sectarian school."

Article IV: The Executive

The first of the nineteen sections that comprise Article IV creates the second branch of government in stating that "the Executive Department of this Commonwealth shall consist of a Governor, Lieutenant Governor, Attorney General, Auditor-General, State Treasurer, and Superintendent of Public Instruction and such other officers as the General Assembly may from time to time prescribe." Each of these officers, save public instruction (selected by the governor) is now elected by the citizens of the state to a four-year term. However, while the governor and lieutenant governor are chosen in midterm elections, providing them a degree of insulation from presidential politics, the others are selected during the presidential cycle.

The powers of the governor are also delineated, with Section 2 containing a key phrase ("who shall take care that the laws be faithfully executed") that mirrors Article II of the US Constitution, which has been used by US presidents as a reservoir of power extending beyond those specifically enumerated in that document.

One of the most specific changes to the 1968 Pennsylvania Constitution came from the decision to create the "team ticket" of a governor and lieutenant governor running together, similar to the national presidential/vice presidential model. It should be noted that, although they were selected separately, there never was an instance in state history of a partisan split at this executive level (though it came very close in the last one held in this format in 1966). The lieutenant governor is similarly president of the Senate; however, unlike his or her vice presidential counterpart; the lieutenant governor is specifically prohibited from casting a tie-breaking vote in cases involving the final passage of a bill. It should also be noted that the most recent constitution eliminated the Office of Internal Affairs. Its diverse responsibilities have been divided among several cabinet-level departments, most notably the Department of State.

The age stipulation for governor, lieutenant governor, and attorney general is set at thirty years. In addition, each must have been an inhabitant of the commonwealth for seven years, with the exception being anyone who held a position in the federal government.

Many of the powers given to the state chief executive mirror those given to the president, such as serving as the commander in chief of the commonwealth, addressing the General Assembly (i.e., the State of the State address), powers to convene and adjourn the legislature, and appointing powers. However, while the governor has the power to appoint cabinet officials, unlike the simple majority necessary at the national level, a two-thirds majority is necessary to confirm in the Pennsylvania State Senate. The governor also has the power to grant pardons (except impeachment, like at the federal level), and, in fact, the lieutenant governor is given the power to chair over the Board of Pardons. The attorney general is also a member of the board, along with three gubernatorial appointees, one of whom must be a crime victim; another must be a corrections expert and the third a doctor of medicine, psychiatry, or psychology. All three are subject to the consent of a majority of the state senate.

The lieutenant governor is also given the responsibility to succeed the governor in case of death, conviction or impeachment, failure to qualify, or resignation. The latter scenario most recently occurred on October 5, 2001, when Lieutenant Governor Mark Schweiker became the state's chief executive upon the resignation of Governor Tom Ridge after his decision to serve as the first secretary of homeland security for President George W. Bush.

Article V: The Judiciary

Unlike Article III of the United States Constitution, which is the shortest of the document, the judiciary article in Pennsylvania's is by far the longest and most detailed. Containing eighteen sections, it specifies the various courts in the state system, from the highest (supreme court) to the lowest (magisterial districts). The size of each court as well as the jurisdiction, boundaries, qualifications, tenure, compensation, and sanctions are outlined in various sections, some of which go into highly specific details. However, what makes this article so lengthy is the attached schedule. This schedule was added shortly after the constitutional convention and provides even more intricate directions for the makeup of each court, including those within the city of Philadelphia and Allegheny County.

Article VI: Public Officers

The seven sections that comprise the article on public officers read as an addendum to the institutions of government previously mentioned. It specifically prohibits any member of the United States Congress or anyone holding a federal office from holding any of these state offices simultaneously. It also outlines the impeachment process, stipulating that the House of Representatives has the sole power of impeachment, while the Senate has the ability to try the official and convict him or her with the concurrence of two-thirds of the members present. The governor and all civil officers are liable for impeachment based upon any misbehavior in office.

The oath of office that all senators, representatives, state and county officers, and judicial officials must take is also specified. It reads: "I do solemnly swear (or affirm) that I will support, obey and defend the Constitution of the United States and the Constitution of this Commonwealth and that I will discharge the duties of my office with fidelity."

Article VII: Elections

The qualifications that citizens must meet in order to cast ballots highlight this article. It should be noted that the constitution stipulated an age of twenty-one, which, of course, would be circumvented by the Twenty-Sixth Amendment to the United States Constitution, which lowered the age to eighteen in 1971. There are fourteen sections in this article, with the remainder dealing with such items as timing of elections, secrecy in voting, bribery of electors, and specifics related to contested elections.

The final section provides the legislature with the ability to establish absentee voting guidelines. These allow absentee voting if the individual is absent due to occupation or business requirements, illness or physical disability, or observance of a religious holiday.

Article VIII: Taxation and Finance

The first of the seventeen sections contained within the taxation article is the most significant. Commonly referred to as the uniformity clause, it dictates that "all taxes shall be uniform, upon the same class of subjects, within the territorial limits of the authority levying the tax, and shall be levied and collected under general laws." Thus, any attempt to install any degree of progressivity into the state income tax is clearly prohibited.

There is also a detailed section allowing the legislature to grant exemptions, such as for places of religious worship and burial as well as public places. Public utilities (not exempt from local taxes), taxing of corporations (allowed), gasoline taxes, and motor vehicle license fees are also mentioned as well as rules pertaining to the commonwealth's indebtedness. This article also requires that the state balances its fiscal budget.

Article IX: Local Government

Rules pertaining to the governing of local governments in the state are presented within the fourteen sections of Article IX. These include home rule, intergovernmental cooperation, consolidation, merging, and boundary change. Also, the three-county-commissioner structure of these governments is mentioned as well as the optional plans available (but which few use) for such government.

Article X: Private Corporations

The four sections of this article make up the shortest included within this constitution. Basically, it voids any unused charter that had been granted prior to 1874; allows other corporations that have accepted the state's constitution previous to that date to continue; permits the state to revoke, amend, or repeal any charter; and provides for compensation of property taken by corporations under the right of eminent domain.

Article XI: Amendments

The final article of the Pennsylvania Constitution outlines the requirements necessary to amend said document. With only one section, those rules are fairly straightforward.

- An amendment can be proposed by either the House of Representatives or the Senate.
- If a simple majority of both chambers approves of the proposed amendment, that amendment must be "published three months before the next general election, in at least two newspapers in every county in which such newspapers shall be published."
- In the next session of the legislature, the amendment must be considered again. If it is approved a second time by a simple majority of both houses, the amendment goes on a statewide ballot.
- The statewide vote on the measure can be on any election date, as determined by the state legislature.
- The same amendment cannot be submitted more than once in any five-year period.
- Separate amendments must be voted on separately.

Figure 3.1 The Process for Amending the Pennsylvania Constitution

Stage 1:
Amendment Proposal Phase
Amendments can be proposed by either the House or Senate
Must pass by simple majority in both chambers in two successive legislative sessions
If Approved:
Stage 2:
Amendment Ratification Phase
Amendment goes to a statewide ballot
Voters must ratify on Election Day

The state also provides for those times when the legislature believes that a "major emergency threatens or is about to threaten the Commonwealth." In this scenario, the proposed emergency amendment can be approved to go on a statewide ballot by two-thirds of the members of each branch of the legislature in one legislative session. Election officials must promptly publish a notice of an election on the amendment "in at least two newspapers in every county," and the election can occur quickly but "at least one month after being agreed to by both houses." Separate emergency amendments must be voted on separately.

Generally speaking, the amendments that have been adopted since the last constitution was enacted have been uncontroversial. They tend towards updating the document to reflect structural changes, such as vacating the office of attorney general in 1980 (after which it would be an elected one), modifying the law as it pertains to items such as absentee voting, and the formal impeachment process. However, it should be noted that as early as May 18, 1971, the legislature and voters of the state had the foresight to add an equal rights amendment to Article I of the constitution. Specifically, it reads: "Equality of rights under the law shall not be denied or abridged in the Commonwealth of Pennsylvania because of the sex of the individual." For a state that is often accused of being traditionalist (especially relative to its neighboring states), this provides evidence to the contrary and, given the time frame, is indeed laudable.

4 THE PENNSYLVANIA GENERAL ASSEMBLY

Image 4.1 Seal of the Pennsylvania House of Representatives

Image 4.2 Seal of the Senate of Pennsylvania

The Pennsylvania legislature was initially established by the state's first constitution, written in 1776. Originally a unicameral (or one-house) body, the General Assembly, as it was known, became bicameral several years later under the second constitution, which was approved in 1790.

FUNCTIONS OF THE LEGISLATURE

Enacting Legislation

Though state lawmaking powers are broad, they are subject to limitations. First, they must conform to provisions of both the United States Constitution and the Pennsylvania Constitution. Second, legislation passed by the General Assembly also requires the support of the governor, or a veto might be issued. In that case, the legislature needs to be able to override the veto, in most cases a daunting task. Third, the statute must navigate through the political system itself in order for it to become law. This is often more restrictive than either of the other two limits.

Budget Approval

Despite the speeches and public pronouncements, the priorities of any government are ultimately evaluated based upon what is actually laid out in the budget. Ultimately, this is what really matters. The appropriation of money and the imposition of tax measures to provide for a balanced budget are the most important functions of the legislature. State monies cannot be spent without legislative appropriation.

Nonbudgetary Responsibilities

In addition to passing a budget, the legislature is responsible for statutory activity in a myriad of areas, such as outlining the laws relating to crimes and punishment, civil property relations among its citizens, the licensing of certain activities and occupations, collective bargaining rights, the structure and powers of state agencies and local government, and educating its younger residents from kindergarten through (in some cases) advanced degrees.

Constituent Services

Lawmakers spend a great deal of their time answering requests posed by their citizens. Some of this contact might come from individuals asking them to support a policy position or someone who wants assistance or a favor, such as a job or a permit. Emails, letters and phone calls are also often received from interest group lobbyists and the members that they represent.

Oversight of State Agencies

Legislators have the ability to put pressure on administrators in the executive branch through committee hearings and budgetary hearings. The latter, in particular, provides them the opportunity to put administrators "on the griddle" about programs and expenditures. Another oversight mechanism is a special investigatory committee. Upon questions alleging malfeasance in an executive agency, the legislature may make an in-depth inquiry into the matter and later report its findings. This process also has the political potential to embarrass members of the executive branch and, either directly or indirectly, governors themselves.

THE STRUCTURE OF THE LEGISLATURE

Bicameralism

The Pennsylvania legislature is a bicameral institution, meaning that it is split into two branches, the state house of representatives and the state senate. Every state in the nation has a bicameral legislature (just like the national government), except for Nebraska, which has a nonpartisan, unicameral legislature. The debate about what is the best option is a complicated one. Supporters of the bicameral system say it provides checks and balances within the government, preventing one chamber from being too powerful since both are essentially equal (although one branch, usually the Senate, might have unique powers, particularly in relation to the confirmation process). Also, supporters hold the view that the bicameral system maximizes representation since a larger number of lawmakers is elected, which in turn may better allow each of the myriad interests that are present in contemporary society the ability to find someone who supports their cause, be it economic, cultural, or otherwise. This in turn also allows constituents easier access to their lawmakers. For instance, it's no coincidence that citizens are more apt to contact their state representatives than they are their state senators for some assistance, a situation reflected at the national level with regards to members of the House versus the Senate.

Those who favor the unicameral model contend that since the US Supreme Court established the "one person, one vote" criteria in *Reynolds v. Sims* (1964), which stipulated that both houses in state legislatures must be apportioned by population rather than geographic criteria, the bicameral model was no longer relevant since it made both institutions essentially carbon copies of each other as far as structure is concerned. This is in contrast to the federal government, where the branches are designed significantly differently, with the House of Representatives based upon population and representation in the Senate equal, with two from each state. Because this framework was outlined in Article I, Section II of the Constitution, only an amendment can change this, an extremely remote possibility given that small states would lose the advantages that they possess in this system. However, if a state attempted to pattern its senate along these lines, perhaps allocating one representative for each of its counties, this would present a clear violation of the court's rulings. Only the national government is able to ignore this one person, one vote criteria, since the US Senate is what it is due to the Constitution; to change it, you would need to amend it. State legislatures are not afforded this protection since their structure is not mentioned in the US Constitution.

Given the reality of that decision, supporters of the unicameral concept are likely to base their case around the idea that accountability is much stronger under their preferred plan. Because there is only one branch, blame cannot be misdirected towards the other house, whether based upon partisanship or interhouse rivalries. In addition, the hope remains that, since individual legislators will be held more accountable, it will improve the quality of the legislative work that they do; they can't simply support a piece of legislation knowing full well that the other chamber will reject it. Nevertheless, the fact that there hasn't been a move towards changing the legislature to a unicameral system doesn't mean that this particular arrangement is dead in Pennsylvania; the makeup of its counties, cities, and, in fact, all of its municipalities guarantee that it will continue to live on.

Size of the Legislature

While there hasn't been a move to change the structure of the system, the same cannot be said in recent years concerning the size of the Pennsylvania legislature, and for many there is good reason. Together, the numbers of legislators in the state house (with its 203 members) and the state senate (which has fifty) make it the second-largest legislature in the nation with 253 members, behind only New Hampshire, which has 424. That state is the only one to have a lower house with more members (four hundred), though five states—Georgia, Illinois, Minnesota, Mississippi, and New York—possess larger upper chambers than Pennsylvania. As mentioned in Chapter Three, guidelines were established at the constitutional convention of 1968. Prior to this, while the number of senators remained steady at fifty, the number of House members fluctuated, generally around the 210-seat mark. The convention also eliminated multimember districts, of which there were a few (primarily in Philadelphia), and dictated that all must be single-district.

As for the exact numbering, it made sense to settle on an odd number since a tiebreaker was necessary in order to establish control. One more than the round number two hundred was agreed upon, and so it appeared that 201 seats would be the final result. However, when it came time to actually draw the seats, there was a miscount, which is why the final total is the more awkward 203 seats. Because of the tiebreaking ability of the lieutenant governor, the Senate remained at fifty. The net effect was to reduce the House by six seats from the 209 that existed at the time of the convention. This translated to a ratio of one representative for every 56,000 citizens in 1968, which by 2010 had changed only slightly, to approximately one for every 60,000 citizens.

The overall cost of operating an institution of this size prompts many to argue that the state's citizens would be better served by having a smaller legislature. According to the 2015–2016 budget, the cost of operating the General Assembly was $330 million. Supporters of reducing the legislature's size contend that especially reducing the size of the House would not only reduce costs but also improve the quality of representation, since the districts would be less homogeneous. In that case, lawmakers would be required to take a broader view on policy issues rather than catering to the parochial interests of their relatively small districts. Defenders of the status quo, however, respond that the savings achieved would be relatively minimal, especially within the context of the overall operating budget of the state. There is no question that larger districts would lead to less direct representation of citizens by their lawmakers. Opposition is also likely to come from those individuals who represent rural districts (and perhaps their constituents as well), since several counties would stand to lose the only representatives who they can call solely their own in the capital. Rural lawmakers would also be impacted to the degree by which they would need to travel in order to serve a larger number of constituents spread across a wider territory.

Of course, it is understandable that one obstacle to changing the size of the legislature (which can only be achieved via a constitutional amendment) is that lawmakers themselves might be more than a little reluctant to reduce their ranks. Fewer seats means fewer members, and some would be jettisoned by the voters automatically while, for those who remained, their new districts would almost certainly be reconfigured, which would cause uncertainty, a condition that most politicians prefer to avoid. The difficulty inherent in attempting to reduce the size of a legislature should not be surprising: according to the National Council of State Legislatures, only five states—Idaho, New York, North Dakota, Rhode Island, and Wyoming—have successfully done so in the past quarter century.[27]

These issues ultimately collided during the most recent effort to reduce the size of the legislature. In 2013, the state house passed HB 1234—sponsored by Speaker Sam Smith, Republican from Jefferson County—which would have reduced the size of both branches by 25 percent, setting the House at 153 and the Senate at thirty-eight members. Smith acknowledged that the cost savings of such a move were minimal (approximately $6 million, according to one estimate based strictly on salaries), and his motivation was based more upon improving efficiency within his chamber. "Reducing the number of members would make the General Assembly, and the House in particular, more efficient in its ability to debate and deliberate legislation by allowing members to have a better understanding of how issues are viewed differently in different areas," Smith said. "It has become pretty evident reaching a consensus with 203 people on major and controversial issues has proven more difficult in recent times." In response, opponents of the bill echoed the issues of representation and access to constituents, particularly in rural districts to which it is more difficult to travel. "Let us not alter the one branch of government that has the closest reach to the people," Representative Bob Freeman (D-Northampton) argued. "Let us retain the easy ability of constituents to personally express their view and have influence directly."[28]

The issue of accountability within a bicameral setting, discussed in the previous section, is relevant to mention at this point. After it passed the House, a number of senators also voiced support for the reduction, though taking issue with the ultimate number of seats to be cut. Senate President Joe Scarnati, also of Jefferson County, pushed for a separate senate bill that would only shrink his chamber down to forty-five members while also eliminating two justices from the state supreme court, four judges from the state superior court, and complete elimination of the office of lieutenant governor. Not surprisingly, the issue was deadlocked, and efforts to change the size withered away.

Professionalism

There is little question that the Pennsylvania legislature is a full-time professional body, and that's been the case since the 1970s. In general, there are three items that shape how a legislature is viewed professionally: salary, staffing, and length of legislative session. Using these criteria, the National Council of State Legislatures grouped the fifty state legislatures according to their structure in a study conducted in 2014 (Table 4.1). The categories they delineated are as follows:

Table 4.1 Professionalism Rating of State Legislatures

GREEN	GREEN LITE	GRAY		GOLD LITE	GOLD
California	Alaska	Alabama	Missouri	Georgia	Montana
New York	Florida	Arizona	Nebraska	Idaho	New Hampshire
Pennsylvania	Illinois	Arkansas	North Carolina	Kansas	North Dakota
	Massachusetts	Colorado	Oklahoma	Maine	South Dakota
	Michigan	Connecticut	Oregon	Mississippi	Utah
	Ohio	Delaware	South Carolina	Nevada	Wyoming
	Wisconsin	Hawaii	Tennessee	New Mexico	
		Indiana	Texas	Rhode Island	
		Iowa	Virginia	Vermont	
		Kentucky	Washington	West Virginia	
		Louisiana			
		Maryland			
		Minnesota			
		New Jersey			

Green Legislatures (Full-time, well paid, large staff)

Similar to the US Congress, the individuals in these states spend most of their time pursuing activities related to their jobs as legislators. They also have relatively large staffs, and their compensation reflects what one would expect from a full-time job. Not surprisingly, these legislatures tend to come from more highly populated states.

Gray Legislatures (Hybrid)

Legislatures included in the gray category are considered by the NCSL study as hybrids. Lawmakers from these states spend more than two-thirds of a full-time job being legislators. Though they receive a higher level of income than those found in the gold legislatures (listed below), it's probably not enough to allow them to make a living without having other sources of income. Some degree of staff assistance is provided, though less than one would expect in a green legislature.

Gold Legislatures (Part-time, low pay, small staff)

The NCSL ranks the gold states as those in which members spend less than half of what would be considered a full-time job carrying out their legislative duties. Of course, compensation reflects this and is quite low. There are a few states that still only pay *per diem* rates. In the gold states, on average, lawmakers spend the equivalent of half of a full-time job doing legislative work. The compensation they receive for this work is quite low and requires them to have other

Table 4.2 Categories of Professionalism

TYPE OF LEGISLATURE	COMPENSATION	TOTAL STAFF	AVERAGE TIME ON JOB
Green	$81,079	1,340	82%
Gray	$43,429	479	70%
Gold	$19,197	169	54%

sources of income in order to make a living. Called "citizen legislatures" by their supporters, these are part-time bodies and are found in mainly rural states.

More specifically, the NCSL study also listed the criteria required in order to qualify for one of these categories: compensation level, size of staff, and average occupation time spent in legislative duties (Table 4.2). Looking at each of these criteria, we will next see why it is clear that Pennsylvania is among the top three professionalized legislatures today.

Salary

Table 4.3 below ranks each of the fifty states according to salary level, and at $85,338, the annual salary for rank-and-file Pennsylvania lawmakers is the fourth-highest in the nation, trailing only those of California. However, it should be noted that the total cost of each legislator includes much more than salary. Other benefits, which include health care, pensions, and mileage, add up to tens of thousands in additional costs per lawmaker. According to one recent estimate, the House and Senate collectively spent almost $4 million on *per diems*, which are work-related food and lodging expenses, during the 2011–13 legislative session. One lawmaker from Allegheny County alone was reimbursed for over $55,000 for this two-year period.[29] One must live outside a fifty-mile radius from the capital in order to collect *per diems*. In addition, members in the leadership also receive higher levels of compensation, and their accounts can be used for political activity. And legislative leadership accounts that can be used for everything from public service announcements and newsletters to—at least until recently—bonuses total tens (if not hundreds) of millions of dollars.

The salary issue reached a boiling point in the aftermath of what occurred around 2:00 a.m., July 7, 2005, when, without any public input, both houses of the legislature passed a raise for themselves, executive branch officials, and state judges. If the "midnight pay raise" itself wasn't enough to inflame many citizens throughout the commonwealth, making matters worse was the fact that lawmakers were able to take the money immediately due to a provision categorizing it as "unvouchered expenses." This was necessary in order to avoid a clause in the state constitution prohibiting members from accepting a salary increase in the same legislative term in which it was passed. That November, even though he had not been a part of the scheme, Supreme Court Justice Russell Nigro became the first justice in state

Table 4.3 State Legislatures Ranked Nationally by Salary

STATE	SALARY
California	$97,197
Pennsylvania	$85,338
New York	$79,500
Michigan	$71,685
Illinois	$67,836
Ohio	$60,584
Massachusetts	$60,032
Hawaii	$59,004
Wisconsin	$50,950
Alaska	$50,400
New Jersey	$49,000
Maryland	$45,207
Delaware	$44,541
Alabama	$42,849
Washington	$42,106
Arkansas	$39,400
Oklahoma	$38,400
Missouri	$35,915
Minnesota	$31,140
Colorado	$30,000
Florida	$29,697
Connecticut	$28,000
Iowa	$25,000
Indiana	$24,140
Arizona	$24,000
Oregon	$23,052
Tennessee	$20,884
West Virginia	$20,000
Virginia	$18,000
Georgia	$17,342
Louisiana	$16,800
Idaho	$16,684
Rhode Island	$15,171
Maine	$14,074
North Carolina	$13,951

(*Continued*)

Table 4.3 (*Continued*)

STATE	SALARY
Nebraska	$12,000
South Carolina	$10,400
Mississippi	$10,000
Texas	$7,200
South Dakota	$6,000
Vermont	$676.56/week
Utah	$273/day
New Hampshire	$200
Kentucky	$188.22/day
North Dakota	$167/day
Wyoming	$150/day
Nevada	$146.29/day
Kansas	$88.66/day
Montana	$82.64/day
New Mexico	None

Source: National Conference of State Legislatures.

history to lose a retention election (Justice Schultz Newman narrowly survived the recall). Shortly thereafter, continued public outrage prompted a repeal of the raise (with only one member, Democratic whip Mike Veon, objecting). That wasn't enough, however, to quiet the masses, and between the 2006 primary and general election season, about two dozen lawmakers, including the top two ranking Republicans in the Senate, President Pro Tempore Robert Jubelirer and Majority Leader David Brightbill, were defeated. Veon himself was also defeated later in the general election.

Staff Size

The second area in which the Pennsylvania legislature satisfies the requirement of being a professionalized institution is in the number of staffers employed by the institution and its members. There are approximately three thousand staffers overall, which makes it the largest number in the country. There is little question that this level of staffing helps consume a large portion of the $280 million operating budget. The number of staffers that each lawmaker receives varies, based on a number of factors such as the chamber (senators generally have more), seniority, or whether the lawmaker has a leadership position. In addition, a number of staffers, as well as those who work for the overall caucus itself, are employed or controlled by committee chairs. The allocation of staffers is dictated by the leaders of each of the caucuses. It can be as high as fifteen or as low as five, with the average being about 10.5 per member.

The evolution towards professionalism can be marked by the increase in staffing over the last several decades. One study revealed that there were only 311 legislative staffers in 1962. The move towards a professionalized legislature was sparked by a decision in the late 1970s to finally provide members with their own individual staff members and district offices, with rental costs picked up by the state.[30] As a result, by 1983, the number of staffers had increased to 1,620 in the two chambers combined. Today, with nearly double that amount, Pennsylvania ranks first nationally in the number of staffers provided to members, according to the most recent study conducted in 2009.[31]

Length of Session

Another gauge of professionalism is the amount of time the legislature is in session. Currently, Pennsylvania is one of only eleven states that do not place a limit on the length of their regular sessions. In the remaining thirty-nine states, limits are established by either a state's constitution, by statute, or by chamber rule.[32]

It is expected that a more professional legislature, similar to the United States Congress, would be an annual, continuously meeting body, breaking only for holidays and seasonal vacations. Annual sessions of the General Assembly were approved by the voters as far back as 1957; however, sessions in even-numbered years were still limited to the consideration of laws that raised revenues and made appropriations in the period that followed. It wasn't until the passage of a constitutional amendment in 1967 that this limitation was finally abolished, making the legislature truly a continuously meeting body.[33] However, although it meets year-round, the legislature is, of course, not always called to order. In general, lawmakers meet in Harrisburg from Monday to Wednesday, which leaves the rest of the week open to work back home on constituent service or other functions.

DEMOGRAPHIC PROFILE OF PENNSYLVANIA LEGISLATORS

The number of women in the Pennsylvania legislature today is considerably higher than it was in the past but nevertheless continues to lag far behind the national average. Using the same period benchmarks utilized throughout this book, research indicates that in 1950, there were no women at all in the Senate and just three in the House of Representatives, all of whom were Democrats. By 1992, the numbers had inched upwards, with three women in the Senate, two of whom were Democrats. Over on the house side, there were twenty-two women in total, with the Democrats retaining a slight majority with ten. As Table 4.4 shows, the number of women in the General Assembly (forty-six) is almost double the amount from 1992. Of that total, nine currently reside in the Senate and thirty-seven currently in the House of Representatives. Overall, the number of women in both is 18.3 percent. While this is an improvement, it nevertheless still places the state well below the median; it

Table 4.4 Number of Women in State Legislatures by National Ranking

RANK	STATE	HOUSE	SENATE	OVERALL	TOTAL	PERCENTAGE
1	Colorado	30	12	42	100	42.00%
2	Vermont	64	9	73	180	40.60%
3	Arizona	19	13	32	90	35.60%
4	Minnesota	44	23	67	201	33.30%
5	Nevada	16	5	21	63	33.30%
6	Washington	31	18	49	147	33.30%
7	Maryland	46	13	59	188	31.40%
8	Montana	29	18	47	150	31.30%
9	Illinois	41	14	55	177	31.10%
10	Oregon	20	8	28	90	31.10%
11	New Jersey	25	11	36	120	30.00%
12	Maine	46	8	54	186	29.00%
13	New Hampshire	115	8	123	424	29.00%
14	Hawaii	14	8	22	76	28.90%
15	Alaska	12	5	17	60	28.30%
16	Connecticut	44	9	53	187	28.30%
17	Idaho	19	10	29	105	27.60%
18	Rhode Island	21	10	31	113	27.40%
19	New Mexico	23	7	30	112	26.80%
20	California	19	12	31	120	25.80%
21	Massachusetts	39	12	51	200	25.50%
22	Florida	28	12	40	160	25.00%
23	Ohio	26	7	33	132	25.00%
24	Wisconsin	22	11	33	132	25.00%
25	Missouri	43	6	49	197	24.90%
26	Kansas	28	13	41	165	24.80%
27	New York	41	11	52	213	24.40%
28	Delaware	9	6	15	62	24.20%
29	Georgia	47	9	56	236	23.70%
30	Iowa	27	7	34	150	22.70%

(Continued)

Table 4.4 (*Continued*)

RANK	STATE	HOUSE	SENATE	OVERALL	TOTAL	PERCENTAGE
31	Nebraska	Unicameral	11	11	49	22.40%
32	North Carolina	26	12	38	170	22.40%
33	South Dakota	15	7	22	105	21.00%
34	Michigan	27	4	31	148	20.90%
35	Indiana	22	9	31	150	20.70%
36	Arkansas	20	7	27	135	20.00%
37	Texas	29	7	36	181	19.90%
38	North Dakota	19	8	27	141	19.10%
39	Pennsylvania	37	9	46	253	18.20%
40	Tennessee	17	6	23	132	17.40%
41	Mississippi	22	8	30	174	17.20%
42	Virginia	16	8	24	140	17.10%
43	Kentucky	19	4	23	138	16.70%
44	Utah	10	6	16	104	15.40%
45	West Virginia	19	1	20	134	14.90%
46	Alabama	16	4	20	140	14.30%
47	South Carolina	22	1	23	170	13.50%
48	Oklahoma	14	6	20	149	13.40%
49	Wyoming	11	1	12	90	13.30%
50	Louisiana	13	4	17	144	11.80%
	TOTAL	1,362	438	1,800	7,383	24.40%

Source: National Conference of State Legislatures. Rankings tabulated by Author.

ranks thirty-ninth nationally. There is a partisan distinction that is present, something that didn't exist years ago. Of the thirty-seven women, twenty-three are Republican, while only fourteen are Democrats. This number of Democrats constitutes only a slight increase over time; however, it should be noted that this study is conducted at a place in time in which the overall number of Democrats is at a low ebb.

Table 4.5 Partisan Composition of Women in the Fifty State Legislatures, 2015

Democratic Party	1,080
Republican Party	704
Nonpartisan (Nebraska)	11
Third Party	5

As Table 4.5 highlights, this also runs counter to the national trend of the Republicans lagging behind Democrats in electing women to state legislatures across the nation. As it pertains to gender, the overall assessment must be that, while the legislature may be home to more women today than it was in the past, it still has a long way to go—both in the proportion of the population and in keeping up with the rest of the nation.

The question of whether women or African Americans have had more of an electoral advantage in recent years is an interesting one. Some political scientists have posited that women should have fewer problems being elected because roughly half the electorate is female. As we have seen above, while in some states the number of women has advanced considerably in recent decades, this trend has yet to truly take hold in Pennsylvania. Others have suggested, however, that African Americans should have a better opportunity for advancement due to the fact that they draw much of their political strength from their geographic concentration, a characteristic that women do not enjoy. Yet their argument does not seem particularly convincing either, in that blacks have fared little better than women in the state legislature.

Again, using the same time frame as the one for women, there were no African Americans in the Senate in 1950. However, there were five blacks in the House, one of whom was also a female lawmaker. All were Democrats from Philadelphia. In 1992, there were three blacks in the Senate, one being a woman, and again, all were Democrats from Philadelphia. Over on the house side, there were fourteen African American members, all of whom were Democrats. Among this group, ten were from Philadelphia (including a black woman), while two were from Allegheny County (also, one black woman) and one was from Delaware County. Additionally, there were two Hispanic members of the House, both Democrats, one from Philadelphia and the other from Allegheny County.

In the contemporary Pennsylvania legislature, the number of black lawmakers in the House (fourteen) is exactly the same as it was in 1994. This includes five who are women as well. All but one of the African Americans serving in the House is a Democrat. Over in the Senate, there are four blacks, one of whom is a woman, and all are Democrats. Overall, the eighteen African Americans in the entire General Assembly constitute just 8.8 percent of the institution,

2 percent less than African Americans' overall share of the state's population. Also, although black candidates have clearly benefited from their geographic concentration, they also appear to be limited by it. For example, of these eighteen African Americans, twelve represent districts located primarily in Philadelphia. Of the other three individuals, two are from Allegheny County, two from Delaware County, and one each from Montgomery and Chester Counties (the only Republican).

There are also only two Hispanic lawmakers in the House of Representatives, both of whom are Democrats from Philadelphia, and one of whom is a woman. This is naturally below the percentage of Hispanics in the overall population. The same can be said for Asians as well; there is only one, a Democratic woman from Dauphin County.

INTERNAL STRUCTURE AND THE LEGISLATIVE PROCESS OF THE LEGISLATURE

The General Assembly is a continuously meeting body that begins its annual session at noon on the first Tuesday in January following elections the previous November. The two-year term is divided into one-year sessions, each with a different number. Special sessions may also be called at the request of the governor and upon a request of a majority of members in both houses. After being elected in 1994, and with a majority in both houses, Governor Tom Ridge, in his first press conference, called for a special session on crime.

The ten-month session provided for tougher penalties, tougher laws impacting juveniles, harsher sentences, and more executions. Special sessions are rare, however, and not always that fruitful. The most recent one, called by Governor Ed Rendell in 2005 to consider property tax reform, failed to produce any legislation. In fact, many of the provision adopted in the crime session, such as laws pertaining to nonviolent offenders, have since been revisited by lawmakers in regular business. The governor also has the option of convening the Senate in special session for the transaction of executive business. All sessions can coincide with regular sessions, though they can only deal with items specifically mentioned in the governor's proclamation. Special sessions are really more of an anachronism, dating to a time prior to the 1970s when the General Assembly met infrequently and action was limited to just the budget in even-numbered years.

THE COMMITTEE SYSTEM

The Pennsylvania General Assembly utilizes standing committees to debate policy, evaluate bills, and perform legislative oversight. The number of standing committees currently in the House is twenty-four, each consisting of thirty-five members. There are also forty-six subcommittees in the House, though not all standing committees have them. Table 4.6 below lists the five contained within the Appropriations Committee. All standing committees contain fifteen members of the majority party and eleven members of the minority party, with the exception

Table 4.6 Standing Committees in the Pennsylvania House of Representatives

Aging and Older Adult Services
Agriculture and Rural Affairs
Appropriations
(a) Subcommittee on Health and Welfare
(b) Subcommittee on Education
(c) Subcommittee on Economic Impact and Infrastructure
(d) Subcommittee on Fiscal Policy
(e) Subcommittee on Criminal Justice
Children and Youth
Commerce
Consumer Affairs
Education
Environmental Resources and Energy
Finance
Game and Fisheries
Gaming Oversight
Health and Human Services
Insurance
Judiciary
Intergovernmental Affairs
Labor Relations
Liquor Control
Local Government
Professional Licensure
State Government
Tourism and Recreational Development
Transportation
Urban Affairs
Veterans' Affairs and Emergency Preparedness

of the Appropriations Committee, which has twenty-one members of the majority and fourteen members of the minority. Additionally, the House has a Rules Committee and an Ethics Committee; these have somewhat unique status in that they both contain certain members of the leadership as prescribed by the rules of the House. The Rules Committee itself consists of the speaker, majority leader, majority whip, majority appropriations chair, minority leader, minority whip, minority appropriations chair, and twelve members of the majority party appointed by the speaker, along with ten members of the minority party appointed by the minority leader. The Rules Committee is chaired by the speaker. Meanwhile, the Ethics Committee is made up of eight members, four of whom are from the majority party and appointed by the speaker and four members who are from the minority party and appointed by the minority leader.

The partisan divide on each committee reflects that of the chamber as a whole, and with the Republicans holding a strong majority in the overall chamber, it's no surprise that it does likewise on each committee. Generally, Republicans hold roughly fifteen seats on each of the standing committees, compared with ten for their Democratic counterparts. As for how many standing committees each member serves on, currently, for the GOP, those who chair committees are likely to serve on two or perhaps three committees, while other members are likely to

Table 4.7 Standing Committees in the Pennsylvania Senate

Aging and Youth
Agriculture and Rural Affairs
Appropriations
Banking and Insurance
Communications and Technology
Community, Economic, and Recreational Development
Consumer Protection and Professional Licensure
Education
Environmental Resources and Energy
Finance
Game and Fisheries
Intergovernmental Operations
Judiciary
Labor and Industry
Law and Justice
Local Government
Public Health and Welfare
Rules and Executive Nominations
State Government
Transportation
Urban Affairs and Housing
Veterans' Affairs and Emergency Preparedness

serve on four committees. However, because there are so many fewer Democrats in the caucus at this time, each of their members are likely to serve on as many as five committees.

In the Senate, there are twenty-two standing committees, and, unlike the House, the number of members on each varies somewhat, as Table 4.7 demonstrates. Also, in comparison to the House, there are no permanently established subcommittees in the Senate, although a chair of a standing committee does have the ability to create one in order to study or investigate a matter falling within their jurisdiction. The GOP also controls the upper chamber by a healthy margin, and so they also have a strong majority on each standing in that chamber, where there are generally six Republican senators, compared to three for the Democrats. Because of the significantly smaller size of the Senate and the fact that there is still a rather large number of committees, members have more responsibility on both sides, as each senator sits on approximately six committees.

Like the House, the Senate Committee on Ethics has a unique status apart from the other standing committees in that the partisan balance is equal between the two parties. In addition, the six members who make up the Ethics Committee, three from each party, are appointed by the *president pro tempore*. The three members who represent the minority party are selected from the recommendations of the minority leader. The *president pro tempore* is also an *ex officio* member of every standing committee except those of ethics and official conduct.

Unlike the United States Congress, there are no joint committees in the General Assembly, though there are, however, ten joint legislative services committees (Table 4.8).

Table 4.8 Joint Committees in the Pennsylvania Legislature

Capital Preservation Committee
Capital Preservation Committee
Center for Rural Pennsylvania
Commission on Sentencing
Joint Conservation Committee
Joint State Government Commission
Legislative Budget and Finance Committee
Legislative Reference Bureau
Local Government Commission
Legislative Data Procession Center

Select Committees

A temporary committee created to study a particular issue or certain aspect related to a piece of legislation, a select committee usually holds public hearings in which interested parties are invited to testify. At the conclusion of the hearing, the select committee may decide to issue a committee report. Beginning in late fall of 2015, the state senate instituted a select committee made up of four Republicans and three Democrats to investigate and determine whether State Attorney General Kathleen Kane could continue to fulfill her responsibilities despite having her law license revoked by the state supreme court.

Conference Committees

When the House and Senate pass different versions of a bill within their respective chambers, a conference committee is formed of members of both branches in order to work out a compromise. The conference committee is comprised of three members representing each

Box 4.1 Leadership Positions in the Pennsylvania Legislature

Pennsylvania Senate		
President of the Senate	Mike Stack (D)	
President Pro Tempore	Joseph Scarnatti III (R)	
	Republican Majority	**Democratic Minority**
Floor Leaders	Jake Corman	Jay Costa
Whips	John Gordner	Anthony Williams
Caucus Chair	Bob Mensch	Wayne Fontana
Caucus Secretary	Richard Alloway II	Lawrence Farnese Jr.
Appropriations Committee Chair	Patrick Browne	Vincent Hughes
Caucus Administrator	Charles McIllhinney Jr.	John Yudichak
Policy Committee Chair	David Argall	Lisa Boscola

Pennsylvania House of Representatives		
Speaker of the House	Mike Turzai (R)	
	Republican Majority	**Democratic Minority**
Floor Leaders	Dave Reed	Frank Dermody
Whips	Bryan Cutler	Michael Hanna
Caucus Chair	Marcy Toepel	Dan Frankel
Caucus Secretary	Donna Oberlander	Rosita Youngblood
Appropriations Committee Chair	Stan Saylor	Joseph Markosek
Caucus Administrator	Kurt Masser	Neal Goodman
Policy Committee Chair	Kerry Benninghoff	P. Michael Sturla

chamber, with the majority party having the privilege of appointing two. The speaker of the house appoints members to represent their caucus, and the president of the senate does likewise. Once a majority of the conferees from each chamber has reached an agreement (if they do), a committee report is issued. That report must be approved by roll call vote within both houses before it can be delivered to the governor for his or her signature. Should that occur, the legislation becomes law; however, should the governor veto the bill, a two-thirds vote of members present in both chambers is necessary to override the veto and allow it to become law.

APPORTIONMENT

Few activities conducted within the confines of the legislature have greater long-term ramifications than those of the redistricting process. Control of both houses as well as that of the congressional delegation are directly affected, and political careers can either flourish or come crashing down due to the way in which legislative boundaries are drawn.

The process for reapportionment, however, does differ for federal and state districts. At the federal level, congressional seats are redrawn after the decennial census every decade by traditional legislative action. That is, the final plan must be approved by a majority vote in both houses before it is sent to the governor for a signature. Should one party control all three actors, they can impose their will upon the minority party and its members. That has been the case during the last two rounds in both 2001 and 2011, when the Republican Party had total control of the legislature and Governors Tom Ridge and Tom Corbett as allies in their position as chief executive. Should there be divided government, which was the case following previous decades, a compromise is ultimately reached, with perhaps both sides forced to sacrifice either a member or a seat.

However, for the state legislature, Article 2, Section 17 of the Pennsylvania Constitution stipulates that a legislative reapportionment commission be charged with drawing the boundaries for both the House and Senate. The commission is made up of four members, those being the leaders of each party in both chambers. Should a dispute arise, a fifth member, chosen by the Pennsylvania Supreme Court, is arbiter. Though turnout was low and few voters across the commonwealth paid much attention, one of the most important elections in recent years was the 2009 contest between two state superior court judges, Republican Joan Orie Melvin and Democrat Jack Panella. At the time, the supreme court was split evenly along partisan lines. Hence, this election would not only impact the balance of the court in the short term as it pertains to judicial decision making but would provide the majority party the ability to appoint the fifth person to the reapportionment commission. With Melvin's subsequent victory, the Republican majority selected Judge Stephen J. McEwen, Jr., a Republican, to be the swing vote. In the long term, this effectively gave the GOP control over the redistricting process for both houses of the General Assembly; this control would hold forth throughout the upcoming decade.

With highly sophisticated computer technology providing detailed analysis of voters' political tendencies right down to the precinct level, and with Republican cartographers holding the mapmaking pen, this has made the Democrats' attempt to retake control of the legislature an even more daunting task. It also needs to be added that there is a natural gerrymander that takes place, which hurts Democrats since a significant portion of their supporters are concentrated in urban areas, particularly Philadelphia and Pittsburgh. This doesn't impact statewide elections since every vote is essentially funneled into the same ballot box and counts equally.

However, in legislative elections, this concentration tends to "waste" more Democratic votes, meaning their candidates, often facing only nominal challengers or no challenge at all, are more likely to win larger victories. Republicans have a similar situation in many of the state's more rural areas; however, there are fewer of them overall. The bottom line is that control of the legislature is more often decided by who controls the swing regions of the state—many of which are found in suburban areas—politically. With the ability to control how those seats are drawn, the Republicans clearly have the upper hand until the next round of redistricting takes place following the 2020 census. It should also be noted that Democrats seemingly learned from this experience, placing an unprecedented amount of resources in the three supreme court seats contested in 2015. Having swept all three, they are not virtually guaranteed control of the process in this next round. Surely, for some Democrats, 2022 can't come quickly enough.

HOW A BILL BECOMES A LAW

During an average two-year term, approximately five thousand bills are introduced within the General Assembly. However, the number that ultimately become law is much less: approximately three hundred (Pennsylvania General Assembly website). Any member of the legislature can introduce legislation. Below is a legislative overview of Act 5, which was signed into law by Governor Wolf on February 16, 2016. This bipartisan effort allows individuals convicted of certain misdemeanors to petition a state court to have their records sealed, provided they meet certain conditions such as maintaining a clean criminal history in the interim and paying a nominal process fee. The short title of the bill, sponsored by Senator Stewart Greenleaf (R-Montgomery), is:

"An Act amending Titles 18 (Crimes and Offenses) and 42 (Judiciary and Judicial Procedure) of the Pennsylvania Consolidated Statutes, in criminal history record information, further providing for general regulations and providing for order for limited access; and, in governance of the system, providing for petition for expungement or order for limited access fee."

Another characteristic of the contemporary Pennsylvania legislature, and one that relates to what was mentioned earlier in this chapter, is how the lawmakers view themselves professionally. Not surprisingly, given how the level of professionalization has changed over the years relative

Box 4.2 How a Bill Becomes a Law: The Textbook Version

Senate Activity	House Activity
Member Submits Bill Usually at	Member Submits Bill Usually at
Request of Constituent or Interest Group	Request of Constituent or Interest Group
Bill Referred to Appropriate	Bill Referred to Appropriate
Standing Committee	Standing Committee
Committee Decides to Approve	Committee Decides to Approve
or Table the Bill (essentially killing it)	or Table the Bill (essentially killing it)
Bill is Scheduled for Consideration	Bill is Scheduled for Consideration
on Senate Floor	on House Floor
Bill is Debated on Senate Floor	Bill is Debated on House Floor
Bill is Approved or Defeated	Bill is Approved or Defeated
on Senate Floor	on House Floor
If Approved on Senate Floor,	If Approved on House Floor,
Bill is Sent to the House	Bill is Sent to the Senate
If House Amends,	If Senate Amends,
Conference Committee is Formed	Conference Committee is Formed
with Senators and House Members	with House Members and Senators
If Conference Committee Cannot Agree	If Conference Committee Cannot Agree
on Changes, the Bill is Killed	on Changes, the Bill is Killed
If Conference Committee Does Agree	If Conference Committee Does Agree
on Changes, Issues a Conference Report	on Changes, Issues a Conference Report

(*Continued*)

Box 4.2 (*Continued*)

Senate Activity	House Activity
Conference Bill Must Be Approved	Conference Bill Must be Approved
by Senate in Identical Form	by House in Identical Form
Governor Has Three Options	
Sign Bill and It Becomes Law	
Do Nothing and It Becomes Law after Ten Days	
Veto the Bill	
If Vetoed: Both Houses Must Override	
With a Two-Thirds Vote for it to	
Become Law	

Box 4.3 How a Bill Becomes a Law: The Reality Version

Senate Activity	House Activity
Referred to Judiciary Committee	Referred to Judiciary Committee
January 15, 2015	February 26, 2015
Reported as Committed	Reported as Amended
January 22, 2015	June 28, 2015
First Consideration	First Consideration
January 22, 2015	June 28, 2015
Rereferred to Appropriations	Tabled
February 3, 2015	June 28, 2015
Rereported as Committed	Removed from Table
February 17, 2015	June 29, 2015

(*Continued*)

Box 4.3 (*Continued*)

Senate Activity	House Activity
Second Consideration	Second Consideration with Amendments
February 18, 2015	June 30, 2015
Third Consideration	Rereferred to Appropriations
Final Passage	June 30, 2015
February 23, 2015 (49–0)	
	Rereported as Committed
Rereferred to Rules Committee	July 21, 2015
October 28, 2015	
	Tabled
Rereported on Concurrence,	October 26, 2015
as Amended	
January 26, 2016	Removed from Table
	October 26, 2015
Senate Concurred	
On House Amendments	Third Consideration with Amendments
January 27, 2016 (48–0)	October 27, 2015
Signed in Senate	Final Passage
February 8, 2016	October 27, 2015 (193–4)
	Referred to Rules Committee
	January 27, 2016
	Rereported on Concurrence,
	as Committed
	January 27, 2016

(*Continued*)

Box 4.3 (*Continued*)

Senate Activity	House Activity
	House Concurred
	to Senate Amendments
	January 27, 2016 (187–2)
Signed in House	
January 27, 2016	
Presented to the Governor	
February 8, 2016	
Signed by the Governor	
February 16, 2016	

than did their predecessors. Using biographical notes published in *The Pennsylvania Manual*, Table 4.9 reveals that in 1950 only one member of the entire General Assembly, a senator, identified himself as a legislator. By 1990, clearly much had changed; the institution was now highly professionalized, and the majority of members identified themselves in that manner. In the House, 84.3 percent identified themselves as legislators, while 74 percent of senators

Table 4.9 Self-Identified Occupation of Pennsylvania Legislators

	1950		1990		2014	
SENATE	NUMBER	PERCENT	NUMBER	PERCENT	NUMBER	PERCENT
Lawmaker or Legislator	1	2	37	74	46	92
Other	49	98	13	26	4	8
HOUSE	1950		1990		2014	
Lawmaker or Legislator	0	0	171	84.3	159	78.3
Other	210	100	32	15.7	44	21.7

Source: *The Pennsylvania Manual.*

viewed themselves as such. One reason why fewer individuals in the Senate were willing or able to identify themselves as full-time legislators, as compared to their house colleagues, may be due in part to longevity. More senior members either continued to visualize themselves professionally the same way they had for years, and even decades, before, when they first entered the legislature, or they simply hadn't updated their biographies for *The Pennsylvania Manual.*

It is intriguing that in the most recent legislature observed, while the Senate has changed in the way one would expect (with more lawmakers viewing it as their primary occupation), the same wasn't the case for House members. The percentage of lawmakers in that chamber actually dropped over the last several decades, though not dramatically. Whether this is just a peculiarity or points to a different type of lawmaker getting elected to serve should be investigated in the years going forward.

5 THE EXECUTIVE BRANCH IN PENNSYLVANIA

FORMAL POWERS OF THE GOVERNOR

As can be said for each of the fifty states, the governor is the chief executive officer of the Commonwealth of Pennsylvania. Indeed, this position within state government largely parallels that of the president of the United States at the federal level. According to the Pennsylvania Constitution, however, the age requirement for governor is somewhat less restrictive at thirty years (five fewer than the president). The governor must also have been a resident of the commonwealth for the preceding seven years, unless his or her absence is attributable to conducting official business for either the nation or state. The term of office is four years, and each individual is limited to two successive terms.

Governors are elected jointly with their lieutenant governors during midterm presidential elections. Pennsylvania is one of thirty-six states, including most of the largest states, that hold these contests during this particular cycle. This is not an accident, as many states prefer this situation because it is more likely to be the focus of the voters' attention. The only race that could conceivably attract more interest is the occasional US Senate race. Personalities and issues that dominate a presidential contest are thus not likely to affect this election, though current presidential approval ratings certainly can be a factor. In comparison, nine states elect their governors during a presidential year, while the five remaining states utilize odd years to select their chief executives.

Image 5.1 Seal of the Governor of Pennsylvania

The governor's formal powers derive from the state constitution, which prescribes that "the supreme executive power shall be vested in the

Governor, who shall take care that the laws be faithfully executed." In addition, powers can also be a result of legislative statute or precedent established by a predecessor. Scholars point to a number of measures that help determine whether a particular state's institutional powers rank their office as one that is weak or strong. The most-cited study was conducted by political scientist Thad Beyle, who constructed an index of the powers possessed by governors according to five different criteria. These include: 1) tenure of office, measured by whether the governor is term limited (and if so, to what extent) as well as the length of the governor's term; 2) executive structure, or how many other individuals in the executive branch are elected independently of the governor; 3) powers of appointment, measured by how many policy-making officials in the state are appointed by the governor; 4) veto powers, which details the conditions under which the governor can veto legislation; and 5) fiscal powers, which calculates how much influence the governor possesses over the state budget. Using this model typology, Pennsylvania is generally ranked within the median of all state governors.[34]

Tenure of Office

The term of office for Pennsylvania's governor is four years, which is the general standard nationally. The only exceptions are New Hampshire and Vermont, which limit their chief executives to two-year terms, though it should be noted that neither places any limit on how many terms a governor is able to serve. As for term limits, Pennsylvania is one of twenty-three states that limit the governor to two terms, though individuals are reeligible after sitting out four years. In contrast, Virginia remains the only state that limits its governor to just one term (though he or she may return after a four-year hiatus). There are eight other states that limit their governors to two terms without any ability to return in the future. Two other states limit their governors to eight years in office within a twelve-year period, while two others similarly limit it to eight years within a sixteen-year period. At the other end of the spectrum, twelve states allow their chief executives to serve for an unlimited period of time.[35]

Executive Structure

Outside of the office of governor, twenty other offices are elected in particular states; positions such as insurance, land, labor, tax, agriculture, railroad, and even highway commissioner are elected in some states. North Dakota, with eleven, has the most, and one could consider the number even higher since there are three land commissioners. At the other end of the spectrum are Maine, New Hampshire, and Tennessee, which only elect the governor statewide. New Jersey was also recently in this group, though this was altered in 2009, when it was decided to elect the lieutenant governor together with the governor as a team. Now, along with Alaska and Hawaii, they have two statewide elected officers. Pennsylvania, which only has three (attorney general, treasurer, and auditor-general) independent of the governor and lieutenant governor elected in tandem, is one of states with the fewest, which gives the governor a greater degree of power.

Powers of Appointment

The appointive powers of governors across the nation are usually best measured by calculating how many department heads the governors themselves can appoint. Pennsylvania's governor's appointive powers are among fourteen states considered the strongest nationally.[36] The governor has the power to appoint each department secretary and heads of other cabinet-level agencies. In addition, the governor has the power to select members of various state boards, commissions, and councils, most of which are subject to only majority confirmation by the state senate. Additionally, the governor can also appoint an interim director for the other three elected statewide offices (attorney general, treasurer, and auditor-general) should there be a vacancy for whatever reason.

Veto Powers

Pennsylvania is one of thirty-seven states that offer their chief executives the strongest form of veto powers, forcing both houses of the legislature to garner a two-thirds vote in order to override. In comparison, six states allow a legislative override with a lower threshold of a three-fifths vote, while six others require only a simple majority—a provision that places the governor in an extremely weakened position in relationship to the legislative branch, particularly when there is divided government within that state. However, even this is considerable as compared to North Carolina, the only state that doesn't provide its governor with any veto power. In addition, Pennsylvania is one of forty-two states that provide their governors with line-item veto powers on appropriation bills. This allows them to pick out particular legislative spending proposals without jeopardizing the entire budget. In the eight states that do not provide this option, governors may be forced to accept many unwanted legislative spending proposals in order to get a budget passed.

Fiscal Powers

The governor is required to annually present, usually in early February, a budget address to the legislature outlining his or her plans and proposals for the upcoming year. Balanced operating and capital budgets are required as well as a financial plan for the next five years. Because of the veto powers available, the governor can line out budget items or request additional funding. Again, a two-thirds vote in the General Assembly is required to overturn the governor's budget decisions.

THE ROLES OF THE GOVERNOR

Chief Administrator

As the chief executive of the commonwealth, the governor is responsible for overseeing the entire state bureaucracy. The expansion of governmental activities over the past half century has enhanced the governor's overall responsibilities relative to the area. If reports of incompetence or even scandal surface on his or her watch, it can negatively impact the public's view of the administration, whether he or she was directly responsible or not. However, the governor is not always directly, or even indirectly, responsible, even though the public might perceive it differently. The Pennsylvania Administrative Code of 1929 outlines the organization of the executive branch. Among other things, it stipulates which positions in the state government bureaucracy are subject to appointment by the governor. For instance, some of the state agency heads listed below do fall within that jurisdiction, while others do not.

Chief of State

The ceremonial aspect of the office is another role that the governor of Pennsylvania or any state must assume. It involves items such as welcoming distinguished visitors from both inside and outside the state, providing remarks at high-profile trade shows and conventions, representing the state at regional or national meetings and conferences, making public service spots, speaking with schoolchildren, or even throwing out the first pitch on opening day of baseball season. Whether or not a particular governor finds this part of the job appealing or time consuming depends upon the individual; however, it does provide an opportunity to connect with voters outside of the policy grinder. It certainly shouldn't reflect negatively on the governor; in fact, a politically shrewd governor might try to make the most of these opportunities that are available.

Chief Legislator

Though the idea of separation of powers delineates the legislative branch as possessing this particular responsibility, often the initiative is developed within the executive branch. This is especially true when there is united government, and a governor usually does not find the resistance he or she would when the other party controls at least one branch of the legislature. The legislature tends to be more reactive in either case. This is most clearly witnessed at the beginning of every year, when all eyes are on the governor as he or she gives the annual budgetary address. The legislative agenda is almost always a response, either positive or negative, to that presentation.

Party Chief

The governor is the leader of his or her party in Pennsylvania. Other public officials, even federal ones such as US senators and congresspersons, are peripheral to the chief executive when it comes to representing their particular parties. That's in part because these federal officials spend much of their time and energy in Washington, DC; that is not the case with the governor, whose home and office are in Harrisburg. Also, while the ability of federal lawmakers to be effective is more greatly impacted by their parties' positions with regard to control of the presidency and Congress, the governor is dependent upon the legislators in Pennsylvania for support. As such, he or she is expected to raise money, recruit strong candidates, and arbitrate internal disputes as a central part of the job. When the governor's party loses legislative seats, it is also a loss for the governor.

Chief of Public Safety

There may be times when governors are expected to manage some sort of disaster (whether natural or man-made) that might appear. The way a governor responds in the event of some crisis (e.g., one stemming from flooding, blizzards, civil unrest, or mass murders) may impact how the public perceives the leader of their state. For instance, Governor Thornburgh was lauded by many for his leadership in response to what was perhaps the state's most serious crisis of the last half century, the nuclear meltdown at Three Mile Island in March 1979.

Image 5.2 President Jimmy Carter touring the TMI-2 control room with (l to r) Harold Denton, Governor Dick Thornburgh, and James Floyd, supervisor of TMI-2 operations

THE EXECUTIVE STAFF OF THE GOVERNOR

Similar to the national level, the governor is able to build a staff to help administer the executive branch of government. The specific titles might change over time based upon the desires of a particular administration, but the following are those that generally have persisted over time. Individuals who serve in these positions are not subject to senate confirmation.

Table 5.1 The Governor's Staff

CHIEF OF STAFF
Press Secretary
Office of Administration
Office of the Budget
Office of Communications
Office of General Counsel
Office of Legislative Affairs
Office of Policy and Planning
Office of Public Liaison
Office of the First Lady

The Governor's Cabinet

The cabinet is composed of twenty executive departments located in the executive branch. This number is five fewer than that which exists at the national level. The most important distinction, however, is that, while the US Senate must approve nominees to these positions by a simple majority vote, in Pennsylvania, these appointments made by the governor are subject to a two-thirds confirmation vote, or thirty-three affirmative votes when the full quorum of fifty senators is seated. Below is a listing of each department, with a brief description of their responsibilities.

Department of Aging

Created in 1978 to advance the well-being of senior citizens in the commonwealth, it is responsible for administrating all aging programs while promoting prevention and protection for these citizens.

Department of Agriculture

Established in 1895, its mandate is to encourage, protect, and promote agricultural and related industries and assist the sixty-three thousand farm families located in the state. The department is also responsible for safeguarding the public against unsafe agricultural products through its inspection services.

Department of Banking and Securities

The responsibility of enforcing and administrating laws relating to state-chartered financial institutions rests with this department. Originally created in 1891, it also serves to protect the interests of the public against unfair fiduciary practices.

Department of Community and Economic Development

Formed via a merger of the Departments of Commerce and Community Affairs in 1996, the DCED is an important tool of the administration in promoting development and optimizing the state's economic base. It is also the prime advocate for municipal interests in Harrisburg, providing financial and technical assistance to local governments.

Department of Conservation and Natural Resources

Managing the commonwealth's parks and forests is the primary responsibility of this department. It also offers geographic and topographic information for state interests. It is a relatively new department, having been established in 1995.

Department of Corrections

Originating in 1984, it is accountable for the management and supervision of the state's entire adult correctional system, which includes twenty-six institutions, fourteen community corrections centers, a host of contract facilities and training centers, and even one motivational boot camp.

Department of Education

Dating back to the Free School Law of 1837, the Department of Education has as its mission to provide assistance to elementary and secondary schools as well as institutions of higher education in the commonwealth. One of the more visible departments in the executive branch, it is the only one mandated by the state constitution, which stipulates that "the General Assembly shall provide for the maintenance and support of a thorough and efficient system of public education to serve the needs of the Commonwealth."

Office of Pennsylvania Emergency Management Agency

First established as the State Council of Civil Defense in 1951, PEMA coordinates emergency preparedness and response activities in the state.

Office of the State Fire Commissioner

Achieving cabinet-department status in 1995, this office, which was originally part of PEMA, is charged with overseeing the training, educational, and operational needs of the state's firefighting community. The birthplace of volunteer fire companies in North America, the commonwealth has overall more departments than any other state in the nation.

Department of Environmental Protection

This department is responsible for administering state environmental laws and standards as well as overseeing the state's various resource management programs and mining and fracking operations. Though its current form dates back to 1995, it has its genesis in the Forest and Waters Department, which was created as far back as 1901. As with the Education Department, governors with different political orientations and philosophies can have a major impact in steering the agency in a particular direction by appointing individuals who share their beliefs to lead it.

Department of General Services

Initiated in 1975, the DGS is the general purchaser of government supplies and is responsible for constructing and maintaining the state's buildings and infrastructure.

Department of Health

This department, which has the responsibility for planning and coordinating health policy throughout the commonwealth, was created in 1905. Many, though not all, of the secretaries who've headed it throughout the years have been physicians. The office of Physician General is located in this department, though it is sometimes considered a cabinet department itself, depending upon the objectives of a particular administration.

Department of Human Services

Known until recently as the Department of Public Welfare, this office was established in 1921 to administer programs that provide social services and basic needs for those who are economically disadvantaged. The department also assists those with physical or intellectual disabilities. With an annual budget of close to $30 billion, it is the largest agency in the state, supporting a vast array of programs ranging from child care to those benefiting senior citizens.

Insurance Department

Originally created in 1873, this department enforces the state's myriad insurance laws, such as those dealing with health, life, homeowners, flood, and long-term care insurance, among others. This office also has jurisdiction as it pertains to implementing the requirements necessitated by the Affordable Care Act.

Department of Labor and Industry

More commonly referred to as "L & I," it was established in its current form in 1913 (though it was an offshoot of the Office of Factory, which dates back to 1889) in order to ensure the safety of manufacturing plants. Among its foremost responsibilities today are establishing building safety standards and conducting inspections while also overseeing worker's compensation claims.

Department of Military and Veterans' Affairs

Headed by the Adjutant General and located at Fort Indiantown Gap, this office originated in 1793, though it traces its lineage back even earlier to 1747, when it was a militia organized by Benjamin Franklin. Its primary duties are commanding the Pennsylvania National Guard as well as administering laws affecting veterans and their dependents.

Department of Revenue

Conceived in 1927, the Department of Revenue collects all of the commonwealth's tax monies from all of the various sources. The office also periodically issues projections on the status of incoming revenues to the state's treasury. The revenue secretary is often seen as one of the leading spokespersons for the governor's administration, especially on economic matters, called to defend its tax policies and budgetary priorities. In addition, the Pennsylvania Lottery is administered by this department.

Department of State

The modern Department of State dates back to the early 1970s and rose from the ashes of the Department of Internal Affairs, which had been an elected office statewide until it was abolished by the constitutional convention of 1968. The head of this department is officially known as the secretary of the commonwealth. As the chief election officer of Pennsylvania, the secretary compiles, publishes, and certifies all election returns. Additionally, the head of state is the custodian of all laws and resolutions passed by the General Assembly and all proclamations issued by the governor. The secretary is also the keeper of the Great Seal of the Commonwealth.

Pennsylvania State Police

The Pennsylvania State Police was established in 1905 as the first uniformed police organization of its kind in the nation. The state police provide assistance to local law enforcement authorities and also have the sole policing responsibilities in some rural areas that lack a local force. Currently, the commissioner of state police oversees approximately 4,300 troopers statewide.

Department of Transportation

Created in 1970 by a merger of several other related offices, "PennDot," as it is commonly known, is responsible for developing and implementing initiatives that can best assure safe and efficient transportation services within the commonwealth. This includes not just highways but also mass transit, railroads, and aviation. The department also oversees the issuance of driver's licenses and motor vehicle inspections. In all, approximately 12,000 individuals are employed within the department.

INDEPENDENT EXECUTIVE AGENCIES

Members of these departments are appointed by the governor, though they remain largely independent of the chief executive. They are also not subject to senate confirmation. In addition, there are thirty-three interstate agencies established to handle unique issues and problems that cut across state lines. The most prominent of these are the Chesapeake Bay Commission (along with Maryland and Virginia), the Delaware River Port Authority (with New Jersey), and the Susquehanna River Basin Commission (along with New York and Maryland).

Table 5.2 Independent Executive Agencies

Governor's Advisory Commission on African American Affairs
Pennsylvania Council on the Arts
Governor's Advisory Commission on Asian American Affairs
Civil Service Commission
Board of Claims
Pennsylvania Commission on Crime and Delinquency
Environmental Hearing Board
State Ethics Commission
Fish and Boat Commission
Game Commission
Pennsylvania Gaming Control Board
Pennsylvania Health Care Cost Containment Council
Pennsylvania Higher Education Assistance Agency
Historical and Museum Commission
Pennsylvania Housing Finance Agency
Human Relations Commission
Independent Regulatory Review Commission
Governor's Advisory Commission on Latino Affairs
Liquor Control Board
Milk Marketing Board
Pennsylvania Municipal Retirement System
Patient Safety Authority
Pennvest
Philadelphia Regional Port Authority
Port of Pittsburgh Commission
Pennsylvania Board of Probation and Parole
Public Employee Retirement Commission
State Public School Building Authority
Public School Employees' Retirement System
Public Utility Commission
Pennsylvania Securities Commission
Sexual Offenders Assessment Board
State Employees' Retirement System
State Planning Board
Pennsylvania State System of Higher Education
State Tax Equalization Board
Pennsylvania Turnpike Commission
Office of Victim Advocate
Commission for Women

OTHER EXECUTIVE OFFICERS IN PENNSYLVANIA

The Lieutenant Governor

The office of lieutenant governor in Pennsylvania today largely resembles that of the vice president at the federal level. However, this was not always the case. The position itself didn't originally exist until it was created under the Constitution of 1875. Lieutenant governors were originally elected independently from the governor. Nevertheless, because the two candidates usually ran in tandem, there was never a case of a split partisan administration. One factor that may have prevented such an unusual and possibly uncomfortable situation from occurring was the sheer domination enjoyed by the Republican Party for much of the next century. This allowed the GOP to roll up large numbers down through the entire ticket. Overall, in the United States today, eighteen states follow this manner, electing the two officeholders separately.

However, in Pennsylvania, it was decided to alter the selection of the lieutenant governor during the constitutional convention of 1968, when it was decided to pair the candidate for this office along with that of the governor. Currently, twenty-five states elect these two officials as a team ticket.

There are several different paths, however, in how the ticket itself is shaped. For the Republican Party, that process is usually fairly straightforward, with the lieutenant governor being selected by the gubernatorial candidate (perhaps in conjunction with party leaders) for the primary. Since 1970, the two have been joined together and are usually unopposed. One exception was 1978, when William Scranton III fended off five other candidates for lieutenant governor. This was a particularly unusual situation since Dick Thornburgh also faced a crowded field, defeating four other candidates for the nomination. Even in 1994, when there were three contenders for governor, the party rallied around Mark Schweiker as the nominee for the second spot.

That pales in comparison to the fourteen-person free-for-all that the Democrats offered up in 1978, when Robert E. Casey (no relation to the former governor) was elected. Though that field was absurdly large, a similar (though less outlandish) situation is generally the norm for the Democrats. Only in 1986, when Mark Singel ran successfully with Robert Casey, did the party have a preordained ticket heading into the primary. In 2002, Robert Casey Jr. did appoint a running mate, State Senator Jack Wagner; however, both were defeated in the primary. The winner, Ed Rendell, refrained from naming a running mate, and ultimately former state treasurer Catherine Baker Knoll emerged from a nine-person field.

Having a compatible relationship between the governor and lieutenant governor is the strongest reason for electing the two as a team. The relationship between these two individuals has generally been positive in the state, though there are exceptions. When Mark Singel moderated his pro-life position during his ill-fated 1992 election to the US Senate, Governor Casey wasn't shy about voicing his displeasure. The lack of support from the popular governor

Image 5.3 Pennsylvania Governors (L-R) Mark Schweiker, Tom Ridge, Tom Wolf, Tom Corbett, Ed Rendell

not only hurt Singel in that election but was especially damaging when, two years later, he was the party's nominee for governor and lost to Tom Ridge. Support from Casey, who was popular among pro-lifers of both parties, may have made a difference in the contest against Ridge, who was pro-choice, though he downplayed that position during the campaign.

As for specific powers, the office again reflects that of the national level, as the lieutenant governor is also the president of the Senate; however, while he or she can cast a tiebreaking vote on any question that might be raised in that chamber, he or she is prohibited from doing the same on final passage of a bill or joint resolution. Though limited from participating in these final votes, this does not preclude the lieutenant governor from participating in preliminary votes when necessary. While this might happen only on rare occasions, there are times when it does create headlines. One such case occurred in November 2015, when Lieutenant Governor Mike Stack cast the decisive vote rejecting a measure that would have eliminated school property taxes statewide. Similar to the federal level, the degree to which his vote was truly independent is certainly questionable; however, as governor, Tom Wolf was strongly opposed to the legislation.

The lieutenant governor also serves as an *ex officio* member of the five-member State Board of Pardons. This played a crucial role in the 1994 gubernatorial race, when it was reported that Lieutenant Governor Mark Singel had voted in favor of releasing Reginald McFadden, who had originally been sentenced to life in prison after being convicted of robbery/homicide back in 1970. After Governor Casey signed his commutation papers, McFadden subsequently murdered two more people and kidnapped and raped a third less than ninety days following his release. Singel's opponent, Tom Ridge, who ran on a law-and-order platform, made it a centerpiece of his campaign. The incident is cited as one (though certainly not the only) of the main factors contributing to Singel's subsequent defeat.

As is the case at the federal level, perhaps the most important role of the second in command at the executive level is the ability to succeed his or her boss, whether temporarily or permanently. After Governor Casey was diagnosed with a rare liver disease during his second term, Singel served as acting governor for a considerable period of time. A permanent replacement was necessary in October 2001, when Ridge resigned as governor after having been appointed by the Bush Administration to serve as the initial secretary of homeland security following the terrorist attacks on September 11th. The current lieutenant governor, Mark Schweiker, filled in for the remaining fifteen months of the term, generally receiving positive appraisals for his performance, in particular his role overseeing the rescue of nine trapped coal miners in the summer of 2002 at the Quecreek Mine in Somerset County. This elevated his profile to such an extent that many in his party urged him to reconsider his previous decision not to seek the office himself later that fall.

In this situation, where the lieutenant governor is elevated to the office of chief executive, the *president pro tempore* of the state senate becomes second in command while also maintaining his or her legislative position. This didn't have a notable impact in this situation, as Senator Robert Jubeliler was also a Republican. However, when Lieutenant Governor Catherine Baker Knoll, a Democrat, passed away in November 2008 after having been diagnosed with neuroendocrine cancer, her successor was Senator Joseph Scarnati, a Republican. This created many awkward and uncomfortable situations within the executive branch, as Scarnati wasn't hesitant to sharply criticize Governor Rendell's decisions, particularly during their annual budget showdowns.

Attorney General

Usually considered the second-highest executive office in the commonwealth, the attorney general is the state's chief legal and law enforcement officer. Following a constitutional amendment approved in 1978, the office became independent two years later, when voters were able to select the individual to fill this position for the first time. Prior to that time, the attorney general was part of the governor's cabinet, heading what was then entitled the Department of Justice. The move towards making it an elected office was in part to ensure that it would have more independence from the governor. Elections for the post are held in presidential years, as is the case with the two other row offices listed below. All three of these offices are for a four-year duration and limited to two successive terms.

The general responsibilities of the attorney general are to:

- furnish legal advice upon request to the governor or any state agency
- represent the commonwealth in any legal action brought against it
- represent the commonwealth in any action brought for violation of the United States antitrust laws
- upon referral, collect all debts, taxes, and accounts due to the state
- administer items relating to consumer protection
- review all proposed rules and regulations of state agencies
- review all deeds, leases, and contracts executed by state agencies
- be responsible for the prosecution of organized crime and public corruption.[37]

Image 5.4 State Attorney General Josh Shapiro

Treasurer

This office was created by the Constitution of 1776, and Pennsylvania state treasurers were originally elected by the legislature. This was amended with the Constitution of 1873, which shifted the power to the voters with their direct election. The individual who holds this position is the official custodian of state funds and the chief executive officer of the Department of Treasury. A few of the fundamental responsibilities include:

- the investment and management of short-term securities
- the receipt and disbursement of state funds
- the deposit and investment of monies and securities possessed by the state.[38]

Auditor-General

Created by the General Assembly in 1809, the position of auditor-general was originally appointed by the governor. However, in 1850, in order to increase executive branch independence, it was decided to make it a statewide elected office. As is the case with each of the three statewide row offices, elections are held in presidential years to a four-year term and limited to two successive terms. Commonly referred to as "The Watchdog of the State Treasury," the auditor-general serves as the chief auditing officer of the commonwealth. The Department of Auditor-General is audited itself by the governor's office. Among the primary duties are:

- reviewing almost every financial transaction of the state, except those of the General Assembly, the judiciary, the State Higher Education Facilities Authority, and the State Public School Building Authority
- guaranteeing that all money to which the state is entitled is deposited in the state treasury
- ensuring that all public funds are disbursed legally and properly
- conducting audits of all state agencies
- maintaining a toll-free hotline as a public service to citizens who may suspect instances of fraud, waste, or mismanagement of state funds.[39]

6 THE PENNSYLVANIA JUDICIARY

The United States possesses a dual-court system made up of federal and state courts, and while the former, in particular the United States Supreme Court, receive much of the attention, the average individual is much more likely to have an encounter with one of the fifty state systems. In fact, the number of federal cases overall is relatively few (approximately one million per year), since such cases must involve violations of federal law, federal constitutional issues, or disputes that arise across state boundaries. Roughly only 10 percent of the total number of filings relate to criminal cases, while the largest percentage of cases are civil actions involving bankruptcy claims. In contrast, state courts handle approximately thirty million civil and criminal cases per year. Violations of state laws and jurisdiction run the gamut from routine traffic tickets to first degree murder and can pertain to either local, county, or statewide matters.[40]

Dating back to a few scattered collections of courts established by the state's founder, Pennsylvania is home to one of the oldest judicial systems in North America. Its evolution progressed throughout the years; first came the establishment of a supreme court in 1722 while the nation still remained under the control of the British Crown. Then, later, the courts of common pleas were formed in every county under the independent constitution of 1776. Additional updates and refinements in subsequent constitutions continued until the most recent update, approved under the Constitution of 1968. Finally, Pennsylvania had what became known as the Unified Judicial System of Pennsylvania, which provided for an integrated system (including centralized

Image 6.1 Seal of the Supreme Court of Pennsylvania

administration and a consistent way of record keeping) and now allowed for judges to be shifted according to the necessities of caseloads. Pennsylvania's most recent constitution also added a whole new appellate court as well.[41]

FUNCTIONS OF PENNSYLVANIA COURTS

Handling Criminal Cases

Criminal law is largely statutory (or codified) law, meaning that the law is based upon the constitution or was enacted by the Pennsylvania legislature. This differs from common law, which is a body of laws derived not from statute but from customs and tradition about what is viewed as appropriate behavior. The legal term *stare decisis* (let the decision stand) is a product of common law and describes the philosophy of basing legal rulings made by judges upon rulings issued in the past. While our national judicial heritage has its roots in common law (with decrees coming from the English kings), it is less relevant today due to the extensive coverage of statutory law.[42]

Regarding criminal law, it is the state rather than the aggrieved party that acts as the prosecutor. Generally, offenses can be divided into three categories. Summary offenses, such as traffic violations, are normally punishable by a fine. For most Pennsylvanians, this is the extent of their involvement with the judicial system. Offenses that are more serious but not major are known as misdemeanors (e.g., illegal gambling or prostitution) and are usually punishable by larger fines or even a short jail sentence. Major crimes, called felonies, include robbery, rape, and murder and can lead the convicted subject to long-term incarceration. In the United States, although some criminal offenses such as racketeering and kidnapping are federal offenses, most are violations of state crimes. There are also some crimes, such as drug trafficking, that potentially can violate both federal and state codes.[43]

Handling Civil Disputes

Civil law relates to wrongs committed by one private individual against another but not considered damaging to the peace and welfare of the community and therefore don't rise to the level that would be considered criminal activity. It also differs from criminal law in that it provides redress for private individuals or corporations who believe that they have been injured. Civil law also encompasses statutes relating to marriage and divorce, custody of children, inheritance, and the conduct of business such as bankruptcy.

Policy Making

Not all disputes in the public sphere are easily resolved; therefore, there might be instances when a court might find it necessary to creatively interpret existing principles in a case that it is reviewing. While supporters might argue that the court is finding what is necessary or merely interpreting, critics might claim that it is making policy and perhaps stepping outside its judicial bounds. However, because the Pennsylvania Constitution, like those of most states, is more specific than the US Constitution, the courts generally do not have the wider latitude and discretion that judges on the federal bench possess.

Checking Other Branches

State courts also have the ability to check the other branches of government, specifically when challenges are brought forward questioning the constitutionality of laws passed by the legislature or executive decisions promulgated by the governor. One example is in the area of reapportionment. In January 2012, the state supreme court rejected the commission-drawn plan and ordered that new lines be drawn, maintaining that too many wards and precincts had been split unnecessarily. Because of the late date, the court insisted that the current legislative boundaries originally drawn in 2001 would still be in effect for the 2012 general election.

Nonjudicial Functions

Rarely, judges may be called upon to perform nonjudicial functions as well. The best example in Pennsylvania occurs when the state supreme court has the ability at the start of each new decade to appoint one member (usually the swing vote) to the Pennsylvania Legislative Reapportionment Commission.

PENNSYLVANIA'S COURT STRUCTURE AND ORGANIZATION

The Supreme Court

In addition to being the highest court in Pennsylvania's judicial system, the Pennsylvania Supreme Court also has administrative authority over the rest of the state court system. There are seven justices in all, and of those, the individual with the longest continuous service is recognized as the chief justice. Each of the justices is elected statewide to a ten-year term, at the end of which he or she is subject to a yes or no retention vote by the citizens. Should he or she be retained, the justice can serve an additional ten-year term. Previously, justices were required to retire from the bench in Pennsylvania once they reached the age of seventy. However, in the fall of 2016, voters across the state narrowly agreed to extend the age limit to seventy-five, a somewhat controversial proposal because of what many considered to be the misleading language of the referendum. It should also be mentioned that previously, in order to assist in carrying the workload, retired judges were allowed to continue to serve as "senior judges" on one of the two lower appellate courts until they reached the mandatory retirement age of seventy-eight.

However, should the justice's retention vote fail, or if a vacancy occurs on the court for another reason, the governor has the ability to appoint a temporary replacement whose nomination is then subject to senate confirmation. If confirmed, this interim appointee serves until the next odd-year election cycle, when the voters have the opportunity to elect a permanent replacement. In 2005, Justice Russell Nigro bore the brunt of the electorate's wrath in the aftermath of a controversial pay raise enacted by the state legislature that previous summer, becoming the first judge in the state's history who failed to win retention.

Judges in Pennsylvania, including those on the supreme court, can also be removed for various improprieties. In 1994, Chief Justice Rolf Larson was accused of improperly communicating with other judges in an attempt to gain favorable treatment for them in their cases. Additionally, he was convicted of illegally obtaining prescription drugs. All of this provided a backdrop during a period of time when Larson engaged in a bitter (and public) feud with other members of the supreme court. Ultimately, the state house of representatives voted 199–0 on a series of articles calling for his impeachment on these matters and several more. One month later, following his conviction in Allegheny County on the drug charges, Larson was removed from the court. In October, the state senate convicted him by a vote of 44–5, essentially ending his judicial career since there can be no appeal of a senate conviction on impeachment charges.[44]

As is the case with all judges within the Pennsylvania judicial system, elections are held only in odd-numbered years, with the parties nominating their candidates in the spring for the general election held the following November. All justices and judges must be citizens of the United States, residents of Pennsylvania, and members of the Pennsylvania Bar Association. Effective January 1, salaries for associate justices were slightly over $203,000, while those of chief justices was a little over $209,000. While the supreme court has both original and appellate jurisdiction, like most supreme courts at both the state and federal level, it generally functions within its appellate powers. The court generally meets several days during each month in hearings or administrative sessions, scuttling between Philadelphia, Pittsburgh, and Harrisburg. The caseload of the Pennsylvania Supreme Court has averaged about 220 filings per year in recent sessions.[45]

The supreme court has four types of jurisdiction: original, appellate, exclusive, and extraordinary. Original jurisdiction is the authority of a court to listen to evidence and decide guilt or innocence (in a criminal case) or winners and losers (in a civil case). The court rules on the issues directly, not on a referral from another court. Examples include "cases of *habeas corpus*; *mandamus*, or prohibition to courts of inferior jurisdiction; and *quo warranto* concerning any officer of statewide jurisdiction."[46]

However, most of the cases that reach the supreme court are those taken up on appeal, whether originating from an appeal that had been directed at commonwealth court or from final orders (such as qualifications, tenure) from one of the state's courts of common pleas. Only rarely, however, does the supreme court review a case appeal taken up from the Pennsylvania Superior Court. Almost always, those are denied, and the superior court decision remains.

The supreme court also has exclusive jurisdiction over appeals from a number of boards and commissions. Examples include the Pennsylvania Gaming Commission, the Legislative

Reapportionment Commission, the Pennsylvania Board of Law Examiners (which oversees admittance to the state bar), and the Pennsylvania Court of Judicial Discipline, which investigates allegations of judicial misconduct. Also, capital punishment cases are automatically referred to the supreme court for final review.[47]

The final power, exclusive jurisdiction, provides the court the ability, upon petition from any party, to take a case that is pending before a lower court if the court deems it of immediate public importance. Only rarely is this power ever invoked.

With a record three open seats on the ballot in November 2015, the Democrats were able to wrest control of the court, sweeping all of the races and giving themselves a 5–2 advantage overall. A short time later, it was revealed that Justice Michael Eakin had received and forwarded what some considered misogynist and racist emails on his state-issued computer. This was intertwined with the investigation of Attorney General Kathleen Kane in her dispute with the state's judicial system (as discussed in the introduction of this book). Justice Eakin subsequently resigned his seat in March 2016 amidst mounting pressure for him to step down. Several months later, Governor Wolf nominated another Republican, Superior Court Judge Sallie Updyke Mundy, to serve as an interim justice, thus bringing the court back to its full seven-member compliment. Breaking precedent, however, it was also clear that she would seek the full ten-year term in the fall of 2017; interim appointees usually are pledged to not seek the seat outright, as it would seemingly give them, as incumbents, an advantage. Table 6.1 lists the justices of the current Pennsylvania Supreme Court.

Table 6.1 Justices on the Pennsylvania Supreme Court

JUSTICE	TENURE	SELECTED BY	PARTY
Chief Justice Thomas Saylor	1998–2017	Elected	Republican
Justice Max Baer	2003–2023	Elected	Democrat
Justice Debra Todd	2000–2017	Elected	Democrat
Justice Christine Donohue	2016–2026	Elected	Democrat
Justice David N. Wecht	2016–2026	Elected	Democrat
Justice Kevin M. Dougherty	2016–2026	Elected	Democrat
Justice Sallie Updyke Mundy	2016–2017	Appointed	Republican

Superior Court

The Pennsylvania Superior Court is one of the state's two intermediate courts of appeals. Originally created in 1895 with seven members, in order to ease the workload of the supreme court, its size was increased to fifteen via a constitutional amendment that passed in 1979. Unlike the more specialized jurisdiction of the commonwealth court (see below), the superior court in Pennsylvania is responsible for a wide range of appeals in both criminal and civil matters, along with appeals involving children and family issues. Also, unlike commonwealth court, the supreme court usually defers to the superior court decision, only rarely taking up a petitioner's appeal of a decision that the superior court has rendered. Like the supreme court, though it is based in the capital, members often travel throughout the state to hear cases, and while most cases are heard by three-judge panels, on occasion they might also be heard *en banc* by nine judges. Salaries for judges on the superior court are approximately $192,000 for associates and $198,000 for the presiding judge. Unlike the supreme court, service as chief judge is not based strictly upon tenure; rather, they are selected by their colleagues to lead the court (Table 6.2).

Table 6.2 Judges on the Pennsylvania Superior Court

JUDGE	TERM	PARTY
Judge Susan Peikes Gantman	2004–2023	Republican
Judge Kate Ford Elliott	1989–2019	Democrat
Judge John Bender	2002–2021	Republican
Judge Mary Jane Bowes	2002–2021	Republican
Judge Jack Panella	1993–2023	Democrat
Judge Jacqueline Shogan	2008–2017	Republican
Judge Anne Lazarus	2009–2019	Democrat
Judge Judith Olson	2009–2019	Republican
Judge Paula Ott	2009–2019	Republican
Judge Vic Stabile	2014–2024	Republican
Judge Alice Dubow	2016–2026	Democrat
Judge H. Geoffrey Moulton, Jr.	2016–2017	Democrat
Judge Lillian Harris Ransom	2016–2017	Democrat
Judge Carl Solano	2016–2017	Republican

Commonwealth Court

Unique to Pennsylvania, the other appellate court in the state is the Pennsylvania Commonwealth Court, which came into existence on January 1, 1970 by virtue of the parameters approved at the constitutional convention two years earlier. However, not only is it the third appellate court in the state (along with the supreme and superior courts), but it also provides original jurisdiction in cases involving civil actions against either a state or local government, regulatory agencies, or an officer of the commonwealth. In addition, the court has original jurisdiction relating to matters initiated by the state against a nongovernmental agency. The court also handles items relating to the election code for statewide offices.

Commonwealth court also handles appellate responsibilities in appeals relating to decisions made by state administrative agencies, decisions of the Liquor Control Board and Department of Transportation, and most local government matters that were commenced in a court of common pleas. Similar to superior court, cases are generally heard by three-judge panels in the cities of Philadelphia, Pittsburgh, or Harrisburg, though they can possibly be heard by a single judge or by an *en banc* panel of seven judges. Salaries for commonwealth court judges are identical to the ones of those who serve on superior court, and likewise, the presiding judge is elected by his or her colleagues (Table 6.3).

Table 6.3 Judges on the Pennsylvania Commonwealth Court

JUDGE	TERM	PARTY
Judge Mary Hannah Leavitt	2012–2022	Republican
Judge Bernard McGinley	2008–2018	Democrat
Judge Bonnie Brigance Leadbetter	2008–2018	Republican
Judge Renee Cohn Jubelirer	2002–2022	Republican
Judge Robert Simpson	2012–2022	Republican
Judge Kevin Brobson	2010–2020	Republican
Judge Patricia McCullouch	2010–2020	Republican
Judge Anne Covey	2012–2022	Republican
Judge Michael Wojcik	2016–2026	Democrat
Judge Joe Cosgrove	2016–2017	Democrat
Judge Julia Hearthway	2016–2017	Republican

Courts of Common Pleas

Originally conceived in the Constitution of 1776, the Pennsylvania Courts of Common Pleas resemble the district courts of the federal government system. As the basic trial courts in the state system, they have original jurisdiction over criminal, civil, and legal actions within their jurisdictions as well as any matters involving children and families. Additionally, they possess appellate jurisdiction as it relates to decisions rendered by magistrates and other minor courts.

More commonly known as county courts, overall there are sixty districts, fifty-three of which solely reside in one county, while there are seven counties whose court systems are combined with adjacent counties. Also, Philadelphia, the largest with ninety judges, is divided between sixty-seven in the trial division, twenty in the family division, and three in the orphans division. As is the case with other courts, judges are elected to a ten-year term and subject to a retention every decade that follows. The person with the longest tenure serves as presiding judge in districts with seven or fewer judges, while in larger courts they are selected by their colleagues. Each district also has a court administrator. The salaries of judges on the courts of common pleas are a little more than $176,000, with the presiding and administrative judges receiving slightly more, depending on the district.[48]

Minor Courts

Minor courts, or special courts, are the first level in Pennsylvania's unified judicial system. The three main functions of minor courts in the state are to carry out preliminary arraignments and hearings, decide whether criminal cases are sufficiently serious enough to be sent to a court of common pleas, and set and accept bail, though not in cases of voluntary manslaughter or murder (when they would need to defer to a common pleas court judge).

Previously known as justices of the peace (a title still used in many other states) and later as district justices, the magistrates in these courts are presided over by a magisterial district judge (MDJ). There are 526 magisterial judges located throughout the commonwealth. Magistrates do not need to be lawyers, though they must pass a qualifying legal exam. Philadelphia's minor court is structured somewhat differently, however. It is called the Municipal Court General Division, and its twenty-seven judges do need to be practicing attorneys, though the two who serve within its traffic division do not. Allegheny County is also somewhat different in that thirteen judges of the Pittsburgh Municipal Court are included within its jurisdiction. The annual salary for magistrates in Pennsylvania is just over $88,000 currently. Judges in Philadelphia are paid almost double that amount ($172,000), though those in the traffic division are compensated a more modest $92,000.

Judicial Conduct Board

Created via a constitutional amendment in 1993, the board consists of twelve members, six appointed by the governor and six appointed by the supreme court. Individuals serve a four-year term, and there is also a requirement of a strict bipartisan distribution of the members. The board has the ability to examine a request from any source, even a confidential one, who claims that an officer of the court has either engaged in misconduct or possesses some mental or physical disability that impedes his or her performance.

If a preliminary investigation finds merit in the charge, the board can at that point decide to proceed to a full investigation, at which time notice is given to the individual under investigation. Following completion of the full investigation, it will either dismiss the complaint or file formal charges in the Pennsylvania Court of Judicial Discipline. The constitution requires that for such serious charges to be filed, they must meet the standard of clear and convincing evidence.[49]

Court of Judicial Discipline

Similar to the Judicial Conduct Board, the court of judicial discipline was inaugurated in 1993 and has the authority to consider the charges raised by that board and to determine to what degree, if any, they are warranted. If so, the court can issue an appropriate sanction. Again, the burden demanded by the state constitution is that the evidence is both clear and convincing. The court is comprised of eight members, similar to the conduct board; half are appointed by the governor and the other half by the supreme court. The term is also the same (four years), while a bipartisan distribution among the members must also be maintained.[50]

Removal of Judges

Pennsylvania judges may be removed in one of two ways. The first occurs at the behest of a complaint filed by a citizen or initiated by a board member. The Judicial Conduct Board investigates possible cases of misconduct. After investigating the concerns, the board has the ability to file formal charges in the court of judicial discipline. This court ultimately can decide whether to impose sanctions on the judge in question; these sanctions range from a reprimand to actual removal, depending upon the degree of the charge and whether it is sustained.[51]

Judges may also be impeached by the state house of representatives on a majority vote and convicted by two-thirds of the state senate, effectively removing the judge or justice from office.

JUDICIAL SELECTION

Types of Judicial Selection in the United States

There are variations of five different methods of judicial selection that have evolved throughout the nation's history. In some states, more than one method is used, dependent upon either the court level or the geographic region. In addition, the terms of office, as well as whether judges can retain their seats, also differ across the various states. The general categories for judicial selection are described below.

Executive Appointment

Popular in the nineteenth century, the "California Plan," as it commonly referred to today, exists in only three states: California, Maine, and New Jersey, which rely on gubernatorial appointment for the selection of their states' judges. In California, the nominee must be confirmed by the three-member Commission on Judicial Appointments, while in Maine and New Jersey, the governor's nominee must be confirmed by the state senate. However, it should be noted that in the twenty-eight states that use elections to choose judges (including Pennsylvania), the governor is authorized to fill vacancies should they occur midterm.

Legislative Appointment

Only two states, South Carolina and Virginia, have retained this method of judicial selection in which the legislature has sole power for appointing judges.

Nonpartisan Election

Attempting to minimize political influence, some reformers in the early 1800s began advocating for nonpartisan elections as a way to select their states' judges. How "nonpartisan" they truly are is subject to debate, as some of the states that utilize this model nevertheless require a judicial candidate to first win a party primary election or be nominated at a state party convention. Pennsylvania flirted with the nonpartisan model for a brief period of time in the early twentieth century before abandoning it.

Partisan Election

The method currently used in Pennsylvania is partisan elections. Judicial candidates usually run initially in a party primary to win nomination. Subsequently, partisan nominees stand in the general election, in which party affiliation is indicated on the ballot.

Merit Selection

Also known as the "Missouri Plan" and named after the state in which it was first instituted back in 1940, merit selection is a commission-based system that entails a three-step process for judicial selection. Although there are many variations in the way the process is used by each individual state, the basic format is similar. First, a judicial selection committee screens and nominates three (usually) candidates for each judicial vacancy. The nominating committee usually consists of both attorneys and laypeople, and perhaps a judge as well. It solicits applications, interviews their top prospects, and ultimately submits to the governor a list of (usually) between three and five names. Second, the governor chooses his or her preferred candidate for the position from that list. Third, after the appointment, the judge serves for a specified period of time and then the question of whether he or she should be retained for the position is finally put before the voters to decide. The various types of judicial selection methods used nationwide are listed in Table 6.4.

Table 6.4 Judicial Selection Methods in the United States

EXECUTIVE APPOINTMENT (3)	LEGISLATIVE APPOINTMENT (2)	NONPARTISAN ELECTION (13)	PARTISAN ELECTION (9)	MERIT PLAN (23)
California	South Carolina	Arkansas	Alabama	Alaska
Maine	Virginia	Georgia	Illinois	Arizona
New Jersey		Idaho	Louisiana	Colorado
		Kentucky	Michigan	Connecticut
		Minnesota	New Mexico	Delaware
		Mississippi	Ohio	Florida
		Montana	Pennsylvania	Hawaii
		Nevada	Texas	Indiana
		North Carolina	West Virginia	Iowa
		North Dakota		Kansas
		Oregon		Maryland
		Washington		Massachusetts

(*Continued*)

Table 6.4 (*Continued*)

EXECUTIVE APPOINTMENT (3)	LEGISLATIVE APPOINTMENT (2)	NONPARTISAN ELECTION (13)	PARTISAN ELECTION (9)	MERIT PLAN (23)
		Wisconsin		Missouri
				Nebraska
				New Hampshire
				New York
				Oklahoma
				Rhode Island
				South Dakota
				Tennessee
				Utah
				Vermont
				Wyoming

Source: *Book of the States*, 2015.

During the early years of the republic, governors and, later, state legislatures made the selection. This was a natural evolution from colonial times, when judges were designated by the king. However, there were concerns that under this system, judges were not sufficiently independent since they ran the risk of not being reappointed should they make rulings contradicting the opinions of those who appointed them in the first place.

With the rise of Jacksonian democracy in the 1830s, however, citizens began calling for a more direct voice in the selection of judges. In 1832, Mississippi became the first state to provide for the direct election of judges. By the Civil War, twenty-four of the thirty-four states that existed at that time had an elective judiciary, and every state that followed, up to Alaska in 1959 (which had an appointive judiciary), provided for election. Nevertheless, widespread corruption, coupled with the progressive movement, led in the late nineteenth century to a search for a better method. Some reformers seized upon nonpartisan elections as an alternative, while others felt that this would do little for a disinterested public or manipulation by interest groups. They proposed a system centered on a nominating commission that would receive applications, interview and screen prospects, and submit a list of those best qualified to the governor, who would make the selection from that list.[52]

In Pennsylvania, a variety of judicial selection types has been present throughout its history. Under the state's original constitution, enacted in 1776, all judges were appointed to seven-year terms by a twelve-member executive council whose members were elected by voters. However, the Constitution of 1790 prescribed that judges would be lifetime appointees selected by the governor. This method was adjusted in the Constitution of 1838, when it was decided to subject these gubernatorial appointees to senate confirmation as well. Tenure limits were also reinstalled during this time for the two levels of state courts then currently in existence: fifteen years for supreme court justices and five years for those serving on a court of common pleas (except presiding judges, who served ten years).

It wasn't until an amendment to the Constitution of 1838 that provided for the partisan election of all judges was approved that Pennsylvania's system of judicial selection began to resemble what is currently used. The Constitution of 1874 continued this model while increasing tenure of supreme court justices to twenty-one years and that of other judges to ten years. However, they would not be eligible for retention after that point. In 1895, an appellate court system was created by the legislature with the installation of the superior court. Interestingly, state lawmakers took their cue from national officials when the United States Congress created the federal courts of appeal four years earlier in 1891. Later, in 1913, elections for these judges were changed from partisan to nonpartisan. This change lasted less than a decade; in 1921 they were made partisan once again.

The state's current system dates back to the most recent constitutional convention, held in 1968. The creation of another set of appellate courts, known as commonwealth court, was the most important change, though it was also decided to change the retention vote date to once every ten years.

Since that time, there have been repeated calls for, and attempts made to move to, a merit system. The Constitution of 1968 itself contained a provision authorizing voters to consider in the 1969 primary election whether judges should be appointed by the governor from a list of nominees submitted by a judicial qualifications commission. However, party leaders conspired to defeat it and, ultimately, voters across the state narrowly defeated the effort. Others efforts have similarly fallen short. In 1987, Governor Robert Casey established a judicial reform commission, known as the Beck Commission, that recommended a merit selection system with nonpartisan retention elections, but that idea stalled. Three years later, reformers came even closer to achieving their goals when two virtually identical merit selection bills were on both sides of the General Assembly. SB 594 passed in the Senate but never made it out of the House Judiciary Committee. The version submitted in the House, HB 941, was ultimately defeated on the floor.

Nevertheless, a number of politicians from both sides of the aisle, as well as organizations such as the Pennsylvania Bar Association and Pennsylvania for Modern Courts, have continued to promote the merit selection procedure for the state's judges. Former Republican governor Tom Ridge convened three summit meetings in 2001 to address the issue, but that effort failed when he resigned from office in order to serve as secretary of homeland security in the Bush Administration. Several years later, Democratic governor Ed Rendell highlighted merit selection in his campaign platform while running for the job and also included it as part of a larger plan to restore the public's trust in the state's government. However, his efforts ultimately languished in the legislature and fizzled as well.

Most recently, however, on October 20, 2015, in a vote that cut across party lines, the House Judiciary Committee passed HB 1336 by a 16–11 margin. This was a joint resolution, sponsored by Representative Bryan Cutler (R-Lancaster), amending Article V of the state constitution by providing for the appointment of justices to the supreme court and judges to superior and commonwealth courts. The bill would also establish the Appellate Court Nominating Commission of thirteen members, who would offer the nominees to the governor. Five of the members would be appointed by the governor (no more than three from one party, and representing five different counties), while eight would be appointed by the General Assembly. Of those selected by the latter, two would be named by each of the four caucus leaders. In addition, half would be attorneys and half would be nonlawyers. Countywide election of judges to serve on the courts of common pleas would not be affected.

This movement has been tried frequently but perhaps is gaining some traction. In March 2016, all of the state's former living governors (Thornburgh, Ridge, Schweiker, Rendell, and Corbett), along with current Governor Wolf, issued a joint statement calling for a constitutional amendment to move to a merit-based system. Central to their argument was the record amount spent ($16 million) on judicial races in the previous year's election cycle. Nevertheless, change rarely comes easy, particularly as it pertains to Pennsylvania's governmental operations, and thus odds are that this latest effort will meet the same fate as previous attempts.

7 LOCAL GOVERNMENTS IN PENNSYLVANIA

Whether it's the police at the local precinct, the teacher at the local school, or the municipal worker hauling away our trash, local governments affect the lives of all Americans, including Pennsylvanians, more directly than any other.

However, the nation's governmental system consists of three separate levels—national, state, and local—but from a constitutional perspective, only the first two possess legal standing. This is largely due to interpretations of the Tenth Amendment, which states, "The powers not delegated to the United States by the Constitution, nor prohibited by it to the States, are reserved to the States respectively, or to the people." Therefore, while the public has the authority to elect their officials, who in turn have the power to adopt ordinances that impact their constituents and impose taxes to support their obligations, they only do so at the discretion of their parent states. While individuals may be citizens of the United States and of Pennsylvania, this dual citizenship does not extend to local governments. You cannot be a citizen of Elk County, the city of Philadelphia, or the borough of Bethel Park.

So while local governments may possess many of the characteristics of these sovereign government counterparts, the courts long ago decided that they are indeed "creatures of the state." This subordination of local governments to state authority was most famously stated by Iowa Judge John F. Dillon in 1868. "Dillon's Rule," as it became known, proclaimed that local governments were "the mere tenants at the will of the legislature," which essentially meant that they possessed no powers except those specifically granted by the states. In 1903, the US Supreme Court upheld Dillon's view (*Atkins v. Kansas*), asserting that local governments were mere political subdivisions of their parent states. Today, Pennsylvania is one of thirty-nine states to employ Dillon's Rule in all of its municipalities.[53] Table 7.1 lists the various municipal types found with the state of Pennsylvania.

Table 7.1 Pennsylvania's Municipalities

Counties	67
Cities	56
Boroughs	958
Incorporated Town	1
Townships	1,547
First Class	92
Second Class	1,455
School Districts	500
Authorities	1,961

Source: *The Pennsylvania Manual.*

In spite of this ruling, local governments almost immediately began to exercise their own political muscle in pushing back state attempts at interference. Unreceptive communities were quick to challenge what they perceived as abuse by state authority over their own interests. This culminated in the home rule movement, a drive to grant local authority more control in dealing with matters relevant to their community. Pennsylvania's constitution was amended in 1922 to give the legislature the ability to extend home rule to municipalities, and Philadelphia became the first to adopt the provision in 1951. The state constitutional convention of 1968 opened the door for other municipalities to make the decision on their own, which formally led to the Home Rule Charter and Optional Plans Law, signed into law by Governor Milton Shapp in1972. With it, Pennsylvania became one of thirty-one states to authorize home rule for municipalities, though several others did allow it in a more limited fashion. The net effect was to shift power from the state level to the sublevels of government (counties and local municipalities) in Pennsylvania. While the power may be limited to specific areas, home rule allows for local autonomy and minimizes the degree to which the state might interfere in local affairs. Thus, with home rule, the state constitution grants counties and local municipalities powers beyond the reach of the state legislature.

Another aspect of local autonomy is the optional forms of governmental structure that are made available to municipalities by the state. Overall, there are six optional plans available to Pennsylvania municipalities under its home rule ordinance. They are listed below in Table 7.2.

Table 7.2 Municipal Plan Options in Pennsylvania

1	Executive (Mayor)-Council Plan A (Department of Administration optional)
2	Executive (Mayor)-Council Plan B (Department of Administration mandated)
3	Executive (Mayor)-Council Plan C (Allows for Office of Managing Director)
4	Council-Manager Plan
5	Small Municipality Plan (Limited to jurisdictions with fewer than 7,500 residents)
6	Optional County Plan (Limited to Counties)

Source: *The Pennsylvania Manual.*

COUNTIES

The county is geographically the most universal jurisdiction of local government in the United States. As defined by the US Census Bureau, there are more than three thousand nationally, located in every state except Connecticut and Rhode Island, where they have been abolished. In Louisiana, they are called parishes, and in Alaska, they're known as boroughs (not to be confused with the type of boroughs located in other states such as Pennsylvania). With just three counties, Delaware has the fewest, while at the other end of the spectrum, Texas has 254, the largest number of any state. Counties also have a broad range in population, with Kalawao County, Hawaii containing just ninety residents, while Los Angeles County, California, is the home of over ten million inhabitants.

In Pennsylvania, there are sixty-seven counties, including Philadelphia, which has the dual classification of being a city as well. Philadelphia is also the largest county in the state, with a population of just over 1.5 million, while Cameron County, located in the north central part of the state, has just over five thousand residents, making it the smallest in population totals. The state also divides the counties into nine different classes based upon population, ranging from those containing less than twenty thousand inhabitants to those with more than 1.5 million (only Philadelphia applies). Note that the complete population ranking of Pennsylvania counties is presented in Chapter One.

Originally, counties in the state were largely responsible for maintaining the local judicial systems and the local prisons. As the twentieth century unfolded, however, their roles began to expand, and they became agents of the state in any number of areas: not just the administration of justice but also maintaining legal documents, conducting elections, and administrating a host of human services programs. In some cases, they also took on powers that are commonly thought of as residing at the local level, such as parks and recreation, planning and zoning, and emergency and waste management. As society has become more complex, counties have evolved, and over the last half century, we've witnessed enormous growth relative to each of these areas. They are now clearly viewed as active providers of services for their citizens.

Functions of County Governments in Pennsylvania

Law Enforcement

Through the offices of district attorney and sheriff, county governments in Pennsylvania are responsible for enforcing the state criminal code within their borders. In Pennsylvania, county sheriffs serve process, provide transport of prisoners, and may provide security at county properties. However, unlike other states, they do not perform traditional police functions.

Judicial Administration

The county courts serve as the basic judicial system in the state. Officially known as the Pennsylvania Courts of Common Pleas, each of these courts has at least one judge who is elected countywide to preside over criminal and civil court cases within their jurisdiction. Magisterial district justices, in some states known as justices of the peace, are responsible for small claims cases as well as handling misdemeanors such as traffic violations. These county courts provide county prisons, juvenile detention centers, criminal investigation units, courtrooms, office space, and professional and support staffs necessary to operate the criminal justice system.

Election Administration

The elected county commissioners are responsible in Pennsylvania for administrating elections in the commonwealth. This includes such items as establishing precinct boundaries, purchasing and servicing voting machines, maintaining a registry of voters, ensuring accessibility for all, sending required notices to newspapers, training local officials, and, of course, working the polls on Election Day.

Property Tax Assessment

Counties are responsible for tabulating the valuation of property within their jurisdictions for benefits of generating and collecting local property taxes. They rely heavily upon taxes based on the real estate values in their jurisdictions; these includes land, homes, and businesses. Local municipalities and school districts also depend, in part, upon the money generated by the property tax.

Human Services

Counties are required to provide protective services for children and youth; mental health and intellectual disability programs; drug and alcohol awareness programs; and services for the aging. Much of the funding for these programs comes from grants through the state and also from the federal government.

Land Use

Counties are also involved (along with local municipalities) in planning, zoning, and subdivision review. They are also responsible for comprehensive land-use planning, stormwater-management planning, and planning for the proper disposal of solid waste.

Public Health and Safety

A number of Pennsylvania counties have their own health departments, maintaining a professional staff to monitor communicable diseases, control epidemics, and manage numerous other health-related items. Other counties work cooperatively with the Pennsylvania Health Department on such issues. Counties also provide 911 call center and response services as well as emergency management agencies, which are responsible for the creation and implementation of plans to respond to and recover from emergencies such as storms, floods, explosions, or any other disasters.

Community Colleges and Libraries

Pennsylvania is also home to fourteen community colleges that offer associate degrees and are based at the county level. In addition, some community colleges serve several counties (e.g., Pennsylvania Highlands Community College), while others are a joint partnership with neighboring counties (e.g., Lehigh Carbon Community College), while still others (e.g., Harrisburg Area Community College) have several branch campuses stretched across other counties. The current community college funding model calls for students to cover a third of the cost of the college's operating costs, participating counties to contribute a third, and the state to supply the final third. In addition, most of Pennsylvania's counties operate or share in the costs of operating public libraries for their citizens. Philadelphia supports fifty-four branches along with its main library.

Governmental Structure of Counties

Nationally, there are three basic forms of county governments: commission, council-executive, and commission-administration. The most significant difference between each of these systems is the relationship between the executive and the legislative powers as well as responsibility for the daily administration of government. The Pennsylvania Constitution dictates the commission, or "no-executive" type, though home rule counties do have the option of establishing another form. This commission form is also known as the "plural executive" form and is used by sixty of the state's counties. Under this arrangement, the county governing body consists of a three-member board of commissioners, elected on a partisan basis. Each of these individuals essentially performs both the executive and legislative functions within the state government.

Under the commission form, both major parties nominate two individuals for the general election to compete for three positions. The top three vote-getters get to advance; thus, the governing party holds a pair of seats while the minority party is guaranteed the one remaining seat. Nevertheless, politics and personalities sometime intervene and disrupt the normal process. After 2007, Republicans in Montgomery County seemingly kept control following the election in which the top vote-getter, District Attorney Bruce Castor, along with fellow GOP candidate Jim Matthews (who was his party's failed nominee for lieutenant governor the previous year), received the two highest vote totals. However, a bitter feud between these two prompted Matthews to cut a deal with the lone Democrat, former congressman Joe Hoeffel. Hoeffel voted for Matthews as chair of the council; this, along with Matthews's vote, provided them with a working coalition for the next four years, much to the chagrin of Castor, who was left to fume on the outside. All of Pennsylvania's counties that utilize this "fallback" arrangement elect their executives to four-year terms during the same year; this most recently occurred in November 2015.

The remaining seven counties have elected to utilize their home rule option to install other systems. Allegheny, Erie, and Lehigh Counties have chosen the elected executive system. Under this format, the commissioner's role is essentially a legislative one, while a separately elected administrator serves as an executive. This setup is more commonly implemented in urban areas, where the issues are difficult enough without having to deal with politics. Though it has adopted home rule, Lackawanna County nevertheless uses what is essentially the traditional three-member commissioner system. Luzerne County, where home rule recently went into effect in 2012, has an eleven-member board, which then appoints a county manager. Northampton County has a similar arrangement, although with nine members. In each, there is a mix of members who are elected in districts and others who are elected at large throughout the entire county. Delaware has a five-member council, with each member elected at large. The Republicans have had compete control since the mid-1970s, when scandal allowed their Democratic rivals a brief period of success. Philadelphia, also a city, has the largest council, with ten members elected in individual districts and seven elected at large. Since each party is limited to nominating five candidates for the at-large seats, the minority party is guaranteed at least two seats on the city council. Of course, Philadelphia also has an executive, though the title of mayor is one that better reflects its status as a city rather than a county.

Beyond the commissioners, most of Pennsylvania's counties also reflected the Jacksonian Democratic model, which provides the citizens a strong voice in government. This is witnessed in the rather large number of subordinate offices (as many as eleven of which are outlined in the state constitution), which leaves the decision to the voters through the ballot box rather than individuals being appointed by an administrator. Critics of this arrangement note that with so many individuals sharing both executive and administrative responsibilities, policy can be disjointed, lacking in coherence and direction. Though voters get a say directly in their leadership, accountability for the latter does not necessarily follow.

Another problem cited by critics of this Jacksonian ideal is that it makes the county government vulnerable to politicization. While this charge is usually reserved for the county prosecutors and perhaps the sheriff's department, Montgomery County Registrar Bruce Hanes set off a firestorm in 2013 when he decided to grant marriage certificates to same-sex couples, which was, at least to his critics, a clear violation of state law. The issue became moot a year later when a federal court overturned Pennsylvania's ban, and later, the United States Supreme Court followed suit.

The eleven county offices outlined in the state constitution, and their respective responsibilities, are as follows. It should be noted that in some counties, even those without home rule, two or more of these positions might be combined, with one person holding responsibility for all. All take office the first Monday of January following the November election the previous fall.

Clerk of Courts

The clerk of courts is the custodian responsible for initiating, processing, maintaining, and archiving records in every criminal case (adult, juvenile, and summary) that arises in the county. Among a few of their other duties, they are in also in charge of recording verdicts, processing bail, preparing motor vehicle forms, and collecting monies in summary cases.

Controller

Also known in some places (including statewide) as auditor-general, the controller supervises the fiscal affairs of the county, including the books, records, and fiscal actions of those who collect, receive, hold, or disburse public funds. This office is also charged with maintaining accounting records, processes, and accounts payable; payroll management; and any internal auditing of the county records.

Commissioners (Three Members in Non-Home Rule Counties)

The Board of Commissioners comprises the top legislative and administrative branches of county government, having responsibilities that are both policy making and administrative. Legislatively, they have the authority to provide certain local services and facilities on a countywide basis and the ultimate responsibility for approving the county's annual budget. Their administrative powers encompass registration and elections, assessment of persons and property, human services, emergency management, and appointment of certain county personnel. They also provide oversight of both these county programs and employees.

For those counties that have not opted for home rule and maintain the standard format, commissioners are elected for a four-year term, with the terms of the three commissioners running simultaneously. In the primary election, two Democratic and two Republican candidates are nominated for the three positions on the board. The three candidates who receive the highest number of votes in the following general election in November are named commissioners.

Coroner

The primary mission of the county coroner is to determine the cause and manner of death of sudden and/or unexplained deaths. These may include homicides, suicides, and accidental (and even some natural) deaths. Some of the other duties associated with this office include identifying unidentified human remains, maintaining death records, and issuing death certificates based upon their findings. When inquests are warranted, the coroner is also empowered to perform autopsies, subpoena witnesses, administer oaths, and compel attendance at an inquest upon threat of imprisonment.

District Attorney

The district attorney, commonly known as the "DA," represents the state in criminal cases against persons arrested in the county. In addition, the district attorney also is responsible for defending the county in civil suits while also serving as a legal advisor to the various boards and commissions. Outside of the county commissioners, and in some cases even rivaling or eclipsing them, the district attorney is considered the top official at the county level.

Jury Commissioners (Two Members)

The primary duty and responsibility of jury commissioners is to oversee and maintain the integrity of the process by which jurors are selected. From a management standpoint, they also have the duty of providing a pool of qualified jurors for both criminal and civil cases. In order to maintain an appearance of professionalism and discourage any political concerns, there are two elected commissioners, who may not be members of the same political party. This is also a part-time position in the vast majority of counties where this office does exist.

Prothonotary

The chief civil clerk of the county, the prothonotary is responsible for recording all such procedures before the court. The office is also responsible for filing a variety of legal documents, such as those relating to custody, divorce, medical malpractice, and personal injury, and it is even responsible for processing passport documents. Pennsylvania and Delaware are the only two states that continue to use this Latin title to describe their chief clerks.

Recorder of Deeds

This officeholder is responsible for recording and protecting legal documents of various types as prescribed by state law. This includes recording, protecting, and reproducing any legal document (such as deeds, marriage licenses, mortgages, and wills) that relate to real estate in the county. He or she also acts as a collecting agent for real estate transfer taxes for local municipalities, school districts, and the state itself.

Register of Wills

The register of wills handles all court-related administration in the areas of marriage, probate and estates, adoptions, and guardianships. With quasi-judicial powers, the register can conduct evidentiary hearings, take testimony, and render decisions on disputable estate matters prior to opening the official record. The register also is an agent for the Commonwealth of Pennsylvania for the collection of state inheritance taxes.

Sheriff

The sheriff is the state's top law enforcement officer in the county, responsible for enforcing the state's criminal laws, serving as an officer of the court, and maintaining the county detention center. More specifically, sheriffs are entrusted to serve the courts, whether it be issuing bench or criminal warrants, licenses to carry weapons, and protection from abuse (PFA) orders or transporting prisoners. They also possess the responsibility of protecting the court and municipal buildings as well as other properties owned by their counties.

Treasurer

The county treasurers receive all fees, tax revenues, and any other monies due to their counties. They are responsible for issuing payments on all accounts and bills owed by the county as well as deciding which banks to deposit the money into. They are also required to produce records of every transaction for the auditors at the end of each fiscal year. The treasurer also serves as an agent of the state, issuing various licenses, such as those for hunting and fishing, firearms, and even for dogs and small games of chance such as bingo.

Every Pennsylvanian is also a resident of a specific municipality, whether a city, township, or borough. As outlined in *The Pennsylvania Manual*, the scope of the functions of these local entities is broad, and they have full responsibility for policy decisions on whether to levy taxes or borrow funds to provide local services. These include services such as police and fire protection, maintenance of local roads and streets, management of the water supply, sewage collection and treatment, parking and traffic control, local planning and zoning, parks and recreation, garbage collection, health services, libraries, licensing of businesses, and code enforcement. Below is a look at each of these municipal types.

CITIES

Pennsylvania has three classifications for its cities. Philadelphia, which is also classified as a county, is the only one to have the first-class designation. Its governmental arrangement more closely reflects that of a city, however. There are overall seventeen members of the city council (one each from ten single-member districts, while the remaining seven are elected at large). Because each party is limited to nominating five candidates for these seats, the minority party is assured of at least two seats on the city council. When a home rule charter was passed in 1952, the city adopted a strong-mayor type of system, giving the mayor administrative power over the city.

Two cities, Pittsburgh and Scranton, are classified as second class. Both cities adopted home rule charters in 1974 that established the mayor as the most powerful force in government. All mayors have broad powers with regard to appointment and removal, budgetary responsibilities, and putting items on the agenda before council. Each of these strong mayors also has the power to veto legislation passed by the council; this veto can only be overridden by a two-thirds majority.[54]

A total of fifty-three cities in the state bear the third-class designation. There are four different types of systems used by these cities: the commission form, the mayor-council form, the council-manager form, and the weak-mayor form. The original system outlined by the Pennsylvania Municipal Code is the commission form of government. In this arrangement, residents elect five commissioners, each of whom is in charge of a city department, to overlapping terms. One of the five is also the mayor, and this individual also serves as the commission chair as well as the head of the Department of Public Affairs. This department includes such offices as community development, solicitor, and the police department. Another commissioner is responsible for the Department of Accounting and Finance, which includes the treasurer and controller (both also elected by the voters to four-year terms). Another commissioner is responsible for the Department of Public Safety, which includes the community health officer, the code enforcer, emergency management, and the fire department. The remaining two commissioners are in charge of the Public Works and Parks Departments. Listed below in Table 7.3 are the twenty-two commission-type third-class cities in Pennsylvania.

Table 7.3 Commission-Type Third-Class Cities

Aliquippa	Arnold	Beaver Falls	Bradford
Butler	Chester	Connellsville	Corry
Duquesne	Greensburg	Jeannette	Lower Burrell
Monessen	Monongahela	Nanticoke	New Kensington
Pittston	Pottsville	Shamokin	Sunbury
Uniontown	Washington		

Source: *The Pennsylvania Manual.*

From 1957 to 1972, cities were allowed to adopt one of two alternate arrangements for their municipalities: either the mayor-council form or the council manager form. Seven cities elected to implement the mayor-council form, which provides for a council of five, seven, or nine members. After home rule was established in 1972, nine municipalities in the third-class designation elected to implement the mayor-council arrangement as well. Under this form, the mayor is the chief executive and doesn't share those duties with council members, as is the case with the commission form. Like the commission form, however, the mayor is elected, along with a controller and treasurer, to a four-year term. As is the case with the first- and second-class cities listed above, under this system the mayor is the chief executive and enforces the dictates established by the council. Similarly, the mayor can also veto items passed by the council; again, the veto can be overridden only by a two-thirds vote. The sixteen municipalities that have adopted the mayor-council form are listed below in Table 7.4.

Table 7.4 Mayor-Council Type Municipalities

Allentown	Bethlehem	Carbondale	Easton
Erie	Harrisburg	Hazelton	Lancaster
Lebanon	McKeesport	New Castle	Reading
Sharon	Wilkes-Barre	Williamsport	York

Source: *The Pennsylvania Manual.*

The council manager form, by contrast, removes the office of mayor as a political force, and all authority is lodged with the council instead. Again, the council is comprised of five, seven, or nine members, all elected at large to four-year terms along with the controller and treasurer. However, there is no independently elected mayor in this system. Rather, a manager appointed by the council is tasked with overseeing the administrative functions of the city, appointing and removing various subordinates. Four cities adopted this method prior to 1972, and they have been joined by ten since. The fourteen cities that utilize the council-manager form are listed below in Table 7.5.

Table 7.5 Council-Manager Type Municipalities

Altoona	Clairton	Coatesville	Dubois
Farrell	Franklin	Hermitage	Johnstown
Lock Haven	Meadville	Oil City	St. Mary's
Titusville	Warren		

Source: *The Pennsylvania Manual.*

Finally, the remaining third-class city, Parker City (located in Armstrong County), operates under a weak mayor-council form of government established by special legislative statute enacted as far back as 1873. This system features strong policy and administrative influence by the council and a mayor with little or no executive authority, similar to a borough. Parker City is the only third-class city using this model.

TOWNSHIPS

The township is the oldest form of government in the United States. Pennsylvania is one of twenty states, mainly found in the New England region stretching across to the Midwest, that use the township. There are 1,454 townships in the commonwealth, covering over 95 percent of the state's land area and home to about 44 percent of its population. They include a wide range of municipalities from a size perspective, from eleven residents in East Keating Township (located in Clinton County) to over eighty-two thousand residents in Upper Darby Township in Delaware County.

Historically, townships provided many of the functions of county governments, but at the grassroots level. Items such as elections of school officials, fire protection, road maintenance, and tax collection were some of the responsibilities that townships assumed at one time in many states, though in Pennsylvania they were generally limited to maintaining roads and bridges. Today, however, these responsibilities have been extended in many ways to include environmental protection, planning, zoning and code enforcement, road maintenance, parks and recreation, police, and other administrative services.[55]

In addition, many states also categorized townships as either "rural" or "urban." In Pennsylvania, this distinction is made by dividing them into first- and second-class status. There are ninety-two townships in the state that meet the first-class status, possessing a population density of three hundred persons per square mile. A number of second-class townships now meet this requirement but have chosen to maintain their current status. Since 1972, twelve first-class townships and sixteen second-class townships have adopted home rule charters.[56]

The governing arrangement for first-class townships is either five commissioners elected at large or up to fifteen elected by wards. All have four-year overlapping terms. In second-class townships, generally there are three supervisors elected at large to six-year terms, though there is an option for two additional members if approved by the voters. Other elected officials include a tax assessor, tax collector (second class), three auditors or controllers, and a treasurer (first class). Appointed officers include the secretary, the township manager (if desired), the chief of police, the fire chief, the engineer, the solicitor, and others.[57]

BOROUGHS

Pennsylvania is one of just three states (along with Connecticut and New Jersey) that, in addition to townships, also have boroughs as incorporated municipalities. Other states such as New York also have boroughs, but they are simply subdivisions of the city (e.g., the five boroughs of New York City). In most states, what are considered boroughs are often called towns, though in Pennsylvania, municipalities with titles such as "town" and "village" are not incorporated entities. The one exception is Bloomsburg (Columbia County), which bears the distinction of being the only incorporated town in the state, dating back to its inception in 1870. In general, one way of distinguishing between townships and boroughs is the presence of a walking downtown community, with sidewalks in the latter. In fact, most of the municipalities today are recognized as cities, whereas at one time boroughs only had to have outgrown that designation. About 25 percent of the state's residents reside in one of its 957 boroughs.

Unlike other municipalities, boroughs are not categorized according to population. Thanks to a mine fire that has been burning for over fifty years, the ghost town of Centralia (Columbia County) has the smallest population of boroughs in the state, with less than ten. Many of these are senior citizens who fought eviction for decades before finally winning the right to stay in their homes back in 2013.[58] The largest, Plum Borough in Allegheny County, has the largest population with over twenty-seven thousand residents.

The governmental structure for boroughs is a strong and dominant council with a weak executive. The power of the council is extensive, covering virtually every activity within its jurisdiction. Both the council and the mayor are elected to four-year terms, with the council's terms overlapping. The size of the council largely depends upon whether districts are at large or divided into wards. For those not divided, there are usually seven council members, while for those that are divided into wards, usually one and not more than two are elected from each district. There are also other elected officers (such as the tax assessors, tax collectors, and auditors) who possess powers independent of the council. Since 1972, twenty boroughs have adopted home rule charters.[59]

MUNICIPAL AUTHORITIES

Unlike the general-purpose governments listed above, municipal authorities are special-purpose governments established by one or more municipalities to perform or deliver a particular service. They can be organized by any county, city, township, borough, or school district, acting singularly or jointly with another municipality.[60] Also, municipal-authority board members are to be appointed by the contributing municipality. However, a municipal authority is not a creature, agent, or representative of the municipality or municipalities organizing it. Rather, it is a separate and distinct entity. There are close to two thousand municipal authorities currently in the commonwealth, operating airports, hospitals, schools, parks, transit systems, and water supply and sewer systems, to name just a few. Many of these authorities exercise certain powers and perform certain functions both within and outside the municipal limits of the incorporating municipality. The Municipality Authorities Act dictates a broad grant of power so that municipal authorities may accomplish the purposes intended under the act in an efficient and economical manner and for the benefit and health of all the people of the commonwealth.[61]

Bibliography

Baer, John M. *On the Front Lines of Pennsylvania Politics*. Charleston, SC: The History Press, 2012.

Beers, Paul M. *The Pennsylvania Sampler*. Harrisburg, PA: Stackpole Books, 1980.

Beers, Paul M. *Pennsylvania Politics Today and Yesterday: The Tolerable Accommodation*. University Park, PA: The Pennsylvania State University Press, 1978.

Beyle, Thad. *The Governors*. Durham, NC: Duke University Press, 1983.

Bissinger, Buzz. *A Prayer for the City*. New York, NY: Random House, 1997.

Bumstead, Brad. *Keystone Corruption: A Pennsylvania Insider's View of a State Gone Wrong*. Philadelphia, PA: Camino Books, 2013.

Carocci, Vincent P. *A Capitol Journey: Reflections on the Press, Politics, and the Making of Public Policy in Pennsylvania*. University Park, PA: The Pennsylvania State University Press, 2005.

Commonwealth of Pennsylvania. *The Pennsylvania Manual*. Vols. 90–121. Harrisburg, PA: Department of General Services.

Daniel J. Elazar. *American Federalism: A View from the States*. 3rd edition. New York: Harper & Row, 1984.

Ferguson, John H. "History." In *Toward Tomorrow's Legislature: The Report of the Commission*. Commission for Legislative Modernization. Harrisburg, PA: General Assembly, 1969.

Greenawalt, Charles E., III, and G. Terry Madonna. "The Pennsylvania General Assembly: The House of Ill Repute Revisited." In *The Reform of State Legislatures and the Changing Character of Representation*, edited by Eugene W. Hickok, Jr. Lanham, MD: University Press of America, 1992.

Hazlett, Theodore L., Jr. 1969. "The Legislature in Perspective." In *Toward Tomorrow's Legislature: The Report of the Commission*. Commission for Legislative Modernization. Harrisburg, PA: General Assembly, 1969.

King, Michael R., and Michael E. Cassidy. "The Pennsylvania Legislature." Unpublished manuscript, 1992.

Lamis, Renee M. *The Realignment of Pennsylvania Politics Since 1960*.

University Park, PA: The Pennsylvania State University Press, 2009.

Mikesell, John, and Cheol Liu, Chancellor's Professor at School of Public and Environmental Affairs, University of Indiana and Cheol Liu, Department of Public Policy at City University of Hong Kong.

Osborne, David. *Laboratories of Democracy*. Boston, MA: Harvard Business School Press, 1988.

Lawson, Kay. *The Human Polity*. 3rd ed. Boston, MA: Houghton Mifflin, 1993.

Lucian Pye. "Political Culture." In *The International Encyclopedia of the Social Sciences*. New York: Macmillan, 1968.

Rosenthal, Alan. *Legislative Life*. New York, NY: Harper and Row, 1981.

Roskin, Michael G., Robert L. Cord, James Medeiros, and Walter Jones. *Political Science: An Introduction*. Englewood Cliffs, NJ: Pearson, 1994.

Smith, Reed. *State Government in Transition: Reforms of the Leader Administration, 1955–59.* Philadelphia, PA: University of Pennsylvania Press, 1964.

Speel, Robert W. *Changing Patterns of Voting in the Northern United States.* University Park, PA: Pennsylvania State University Press, 1998.

Sorauf, Frank J. *Party and Representation.* New York, NY: Atherton Press, 1963.

Treadway, Jack. *Elections in Pennsylvania.* University Park, PA: Pennsylvania State University Press, 2005.

Weber, Michael. *Don't Call Me Boss: David Lawrence, Pittsburgh's Renaissance Mayor.* Pittsburgh, PA: University of Pittsburgh Press, 1988.

Wise, Sidney. *The Legislative Process in Pennsylvania.* 2nd ed. Harrisburg, PA: Commonwealth of Pennsylvania, 1984.

Woods and Poole Economics, Inc. *State Profile: Pennsylvania and Delaware.*

Washington, DC: Woods and Poole Economics, Inc, 1990.

Woshinsky, Oliver H. *Culture and Politics: An Introduction to Mass and Elite Political Behavior.* Englewood, NJ: Prentice-Hall, 1995.

Notes

1. Lucian Pye, "Political Culture," in *The International Encyclopedia of the Social Sciences* (New York: Macmillan, 1968).
2. Daniel J. Elazar, *American Federalism: A View from the States*, 3rd edition (New York: Harper & Row, 1984).
3. John Mikesell, Chancellor's Professor at School of Public and Environmental Affairs, University of Indiana and Cheol Liu, Department of Public Policy at City University of Hong Kong.
4. Paul M. Beers, *Pennsylvania Politics, Today and Yesterday* (University Park, PA: Penn State Press, 1978).
5. Ibid.
6. Brad Bumstead, *Keystone Corruption: A Pennsylvania Insider's View of a State Gone Wrong* (Philadelphia, PA: Camino Books, 2013).
7.
8. Pew Research Center, http://www.pewresearch.org.
9. *Governing* magazine, http://www.governing.com/mag.
10. The Center for Educational Reform, https://www.edreform.com.
11. Commonwealth of Pennsylvania, *The Pennsylvania Manual* (Harrisburg, PA: Department of General Services. 2013).
12. Ibid.
13. The Nielsen Company, http://www.nielsen.com/us/en.html.
14. Mondo Code, LLC, http://www.mondocode.com.
15. Commonwealth of Pennsylvania, *The Pennsylvania Manual* (Harrisburg, PA: Department of General Services. 2013).
16. United States Department of Commerce, Washington DC.
17. David Osbourne, *Laboratories of Democracy* (Boston, MA: Harvard Business School Press, 1988).
18. Woods and Poole Economics, Inc., *State Profile, Pennsylvania and Delaware* (Washington, DC: Woods and Poole Economics, Inc. 1990).
19. Pennsylvania Department of Agriculture, Harrisburg, PA, http://www.agriculture.pa.gov.
20. *Huffington Post*, March 15, 2013.
21. Theodore Hazlett, Jr., "The Legislature in Perspective," in *Toward Tomorrow's Legislature: The Report of the Commission*, Commission for Legislative Modernization, Harrisburg, PA: General Assembly, 1969.
22. Michael R. King and Michael E. Cassidy, "The Pennsylvania Legislature" (unpublished manuscript, 1992).
23. Pennsylvania Historical and Museum Commission, http://www.phmc.pa.gov.
24. John H. Ferguson, "History," in *Toward Tomorrow's Legislature: The Report of the Commission*, Commission for Legislative Modernization, Harrisburg, PA: General Assembly, 1969.
25. Ibid.
26. Frank J. Sorauf, *Party and Representation* (New York, NY: Atherton Press, 1963).
27. PennLive, http://www.pennlive.com, June 6, 2004.

28. Politicspa, http://politicspa.com, December 17, 2013.
29. Ibid.
30. Charles E. Greenawalt III and G. Terry Madonna, "The Pennsylvania General Assembly: The House of Ill Repute Revisited," in *The Reform of State Legislatures and the Changing Character of Representation*, ed. Eugene W. Hickok Jr. (Lanham, MD: University Press of America, 1992).
31. National Council of State Legislatures, http://www.ncsl.org.
32. Ibid.
33. Alan Rosenthal, *Legislative Life* (New York, NY: Harper and Row, 1981).
34. Thad Beyle, *The Governors* (Durham, NC: Duke University Press, 1983).
35. National Governors Association, http://www.nga.org.
36. *The Book of the States*, Council of State Governments, http://www.csg.org.
37. Commonwealth of Pennsylvania, *The Pennsylvania Manual.*
38. Ibid.
39. Ibid.
40. United States Department of Justice, Washington DC.
41. Commonwealth of Pennsylvania, *The Pennsylvania Manual.*
42. Kay Lawson, *The Human Polity*, 3rd ed. (Boston, MA: Houghton Mifflin, 1993).
43. Michael G. Roskin, Robert L. Cord, James Medeiros, and Walter Jones, *Political Science: An Introduction* (Englewood Cliffs, NJ: Pearson, 1994).
44. John M. Baer, *On the Front Lines of Pennsylvania Politics* (Charleston, SC: The History Press, 2012).
45. The Unified Judicial System of Pennsylvania, http://www.pacourts.com.
46. Commonwealth of Pennsylvania, *The Pennsylvania Manual.*
47. Ibid.
48. Ibid.
49. Ibid.
50. Ibid.
51. Commonwealth of Pennsylvania, *The Pennsylvania Manual.*
52. National Center for State Courts, http://www.ncsc.org.
53. The National League of Cities, http://www.nlc.org.
54. Commonwealth of Pennsylvania, *The Pennsylvania Manual.*
55. Pennsylvania Association of Township Supervisors, http://www.psats.org.
56. Commonwealth of Pennsylvania, *The Pennsylvania Manual.*
57. Ibid.
58. PennLive, http://www.pennlive.com, October 30, 2013.
59. Commonwealth of Pennsylvania, *The Pennsylvania Manual.*
60. Ibid.
61. Pennsylvania Local Government Commission, *Pennsylvania Legislator's Municipal Deskbook*, 4th ed., 2014, http://www.lgc.state.pa.us/download.cfm?file=/Reports/deskbook14/complete_fourth_edition.pdf.

Index

CPSIA information can be obtained
at www.ICGtesting.com
Printed in the USA
LVHW021933230821
695919LV00003B/15

9 781516 501588